CLOUD WALKING

A Spiritual Diary

By Steven Charleston

RED MOON PUBLICATIONS
Oklahoma City, OK 73120

Cover Art by Suzanne Charleston, www.suzanneartist.com
Book Layout by Lana B. Callahan, www.lbsdesignstudio.com

Copyright © 2013 by Red Moon Publications

Library of Congress Catalog Card Number: 2013901780

ISBN 978-0-9851419-2-9

Printed in the United States of America

I rise every morning before dawn to meditate and pray. In 2011 I began writing down the words and images that came to me during this time. I wrote them on my Facebook page. I wrote them every day except Saturday when I invited people to send me their prayer requests. At first, only a handful of people saw them. By word of mouth, one by one, more people discovered them. Today thousands of people read them all over the world. These are people from many different faith traditions. They are from every ethnic and cultural community. From the messages I have received I know that somehow these little meditations speak to people and help them. For that I am very grateful. I hope it is true for you too. This experience is a mystery to me except for one thing: I have come to understand that while I wrote this book, I am not its author.

JANUARY

January 1

All marks of time are an illusion, but even illusions have their place, so I step over this threshold, with a reminder of God's timeless grace. May the days ahead bring you the challenge to be who you are called to be. May they offer you a warm hand of healing when you hurt, strength in every struggle, the sheer joy of new discovery. May you know the peace that passes understanding, the hope that lifts your spirit to new horizons. May you know love. May your talent be tested. And may the paths you follow, the causes you embrace, the truths you tell, bring you closer to the meaning of your tomorrow.

January 2

We should respect our elders, not out of sentiment, but out of an understanding that the capacity for us to do something spiritually profound never ends. Each of us never knows if in the hour to come we may be called on to be the agent of God. We can turn the corner at any age to discover God's destiny before us. I have seen human beings taking their last breath do more for the living gathered around them than I could ever hope to do. The world sees only the outer shell and honors strength of body. We see the inner soul and honor strength of spirit. And that strength never fades. Never.

January 3

Pride is a garden gate that swings on hinges of humility, to open us to a world with others, or to close us inside with only ourselves. For many of us, we need to swing that gate wide. We need to step out into life with confidence, claim our identities with pride in what God has made. For the few, the garden is an illusion because in our vanity we hear nothing, see only our own reflection, and imagine we are better than what God designed. For those timid in pride, let my prayer open the gate to let their love be released. For the prideful, let my prayer open the gate that humility may come within.

January 4

Softly comes the Spirit, slipping past our defenses. Like campfire smoke she fixes on the one she wants. She shadows our every move. She trails the reluctant hero. She chases the silent sage. In the end, evasion is a waste of time. Like smoke she will curl around us while we become what we can be. She is there if we live up to what we hope and there if we give in to what we fear. Either way, she will be there. Like smoke from a fire burning bright through the night, a sign and a comfort.

J a n u a r y   5

But say the word and I will be healed. What is that word for you? Is it a word of forgiveness? Of affirmation? Of love? For each of us there is a word we long to hear. A healing word that has the power to change our lives. What is that word for you? I pray you hear it. And more, I pray you remember that such a word of grace is the gift you have for another. Someone waits for you to speak. Release the word within, receive the word without: learn the language that unbinds us all through the Word that makes all things whole.

J a n u a r y   6

You cannot see God and live, that was the ancient caution, the one that turned the hair of Moses to snow. But then again, you cannot not see God and live, for without a vision the people perish says the ancient Book. So we are caught between what we may never be and what we must always have. The spiritual reality is not a placid place, but a world crackling with the electric presence of the holy. It burns bushes and withers fig trees, it changes the very substance of life, it drives those who see it to do things they would never have imagined. Behold the face of God and you will see how God beholds you.

January 8

God be with me in my routine today. Be present in my life when I stack the dishes, clean the toilets, vacuum the carpet. Stand beside me at the gas pump and in the grocery line. Watch over me in a traffic jam, keep me company while I do the laundry. Let me not imagine that I can only find you in the serene places of my worship, but worship you in the simple places of my chore filled day. Be my twenty-four God. Be in all that I say and do. Make me mindful that you are there in the most humble moments, the all too human times, when my labor is an echo of my love.

January 9

We are in a turning time. We cannot name it more clearly. We cannot know its direction or its destination, but we feel it. With the deep sense of the spirit, we feel it. The ground beneath us shifts. What has been familiar seems uncertain. Something is coming. Our instincts tell us what our reason cannot control. It is a turning time. The long arc of history bending under weight of chance and choice. Do not fear it, but guide it. Now is the moment to bring faith to bear, now is why we are here. Let us pray this change to the light and make this hour holy with all the witness at our command.

January 10

G ive me one more day, dear God, for my mind to learn what my heart already knows. One more day to wake and know there is life within me. One more day to see the ones I love, to hear their voices, to feel their touch. Give me one more day to watch the Earth do its work of endless change, to see the faces of so many pass me by, to let my senses reach out to breathe in all there is for me to experience, even in just one day. Give me one more day to value one day, any day, for the great gift it is. And let my spirit fly, un-caged by careless time, before the setting of the sun.

January 11

W ill you stand with me to sing, sing the song of our salvation, sing the midnight choir against the darkest night? Makes no difference what voice you have, reedy with age like mine, or soaring in the clear tones of heaven, for when joined in the hymn of our hope, the sound itself raises the heads of angels to listen. Will you sing with me? Sing down gloom and despair, the fear and the sorrow, and sing out the healing vision of every human heart that longs to know its life has mattered, its dream has never been in vain. Sing for our children. Sing for our future. Sing to our God. Will you stand with me to sing?

January 12

So often our lives come down to a choice. Do I say this? Or do I say that? Or say nothing at all? Do I go this way, that way, or stay very still? Like a patchwork quilt, the choices we make stitch our lives into a pattern. Some we celebrate, some we regret, some we rarely remember, but they all define us. They are the moments of our own creation, far more powerful than all the public roles we play. They are when faith becomes the balance and truth the undiscovered direction. Take this pocket prayer with you, for one day you will use it and rejoice: God be with in what I do, God help me make a choice.

January 13

Two of the greatest spiritual teachers on Earth have no degrees, no ordinations, no titles. They are the poorest woman and man on this planet who still have not lost hope. Though I cannot name them, I can acknowledge them. I can honor them, for somewhere, they both exist. They wake up to struggle, to overwhelming struggle, and yet they wake with faith in their hearts. They continue to believe. They continue to live in dignity. I pray this day for them both, and all their sisters and brothers, and show my respect with a vow to stand with them in the struggle against poverty, for as long as I live.

January 15

Where were you when you felt it? Where were you when you knew you were standing on holy ground? For some of us it has been within, in a place long hallowed by human prayer. For some, it has been without, in a place natural to the Earth. Either way, the air is static with the energy of the sacred. You can feel that the walls are infused with the echoes of ten thousand prayers, those who have gone before almost visible in the shadows. You can see the majesty of God in a creation that seems to look back as we stand in awe before it. Where is your holy ground? The waiting room of God.

January 16

I have a radical notion, counter cultural, but grounded in the Scriptures: don't be afraid of your dreams. Many times people have whispered to me that they have sacred dreams, but do not openly speak of them. While I cannot change the Western world that inhibits dreamers and scorns visionaries, I can encourage us to reclaim our right to dream. If at night you have received a message intended to heal or help this world, you are not alone. The voice of one such dreamer still beckons us to look beyond what empire permits to see what God envisions.

January 17

When I was ordained a priest, on a South Dakota night long ago, my parents drove up from Oklahoma, in a car loaded with blankets. With baskets and key chains and baubles. After the service we did a give-away, a gift for all who came. In Native tradition you mark your special moments, not by what you may receive, but by what you have to give. However small or simple, you give. Generosity is a key. It unlocks the soul. It opens the door that encloses the heart. It makes the one become the many. Join me in a give-away. Today honor your calling by giving your love to another. Unlock yourself.

January 18

The search goes on. How strange to ply the seeker's trade, how wondrous and mundane. How I came to this I am not sure, but now it seems like breathing. A prospector, mad beneath the sun, I dig within mountains of mystery, walk the shrouded valleys. I chase shadows. I talk with the wind. I sleep to be in what is real, I wake to live a dream. And just when I decide to give it up, to turn away and find my place behind walls of safety, I hear that familiar whisper, and dare the wild desert to embrace me. How I came to this I am not sure, never sure, only faithful to curious nature. The search goes on.

January 19

I find it ironic that our friends who say we are delusional for believing in God are able to carry on in a world where presidents say there is no global warming, where nations still operate on the idea that if we kill enough people they will believe in our way of life, where a system continues to work that allows a few people to spend millions on a new home while children die of hunger, and where color can define destiny. How delusional is all of that? But still, on we go. No offense, but who is kidding themselves here: those who believe in an unseen good or those who think this is as good as it gets?

January 20

It comes with the territory. Compassion for another so deep it almost hurts, but only prayers to bind their wounds. Love that longs to embrace a thousand souls, but so little time to reach them. Injustice so clear it can mock the throne of truth, but only a few to stand against it. It is not easy to practice faith. The needs are so many, the resources so few. Patient resolve, common sense, a trust in hope unbending: these are tools of the trade and the trade seems never ending. But the reward of a single smile makes it worth a life living. One captive free unchains every heart.

January 22

Please God, be there in every season I inhabit. Be there when I am youthful in imagination, searching for insight, seeking new ground in which to grow. Be there when I bask in bright success, lazy in your love, resting so deeply that even my worries slumber. Be there in the chill days, when I am alert to change, drawn inward in reflection beneath the golden trees. And most of all, be there in the passing times, the dying times, when your hearth becomes my sanctuary, your warmth a promise of my renewal. Please God, be there in every season I inhabit.

January 23

You have made a difference in my life. In many lives and I want to thank you. Thank you on behalf of us all. You may not know us, not know our stories, our secret fears or public longings, but you have touched us as though you knew. You have given us a reason to hope because you have shown us there is something real to believe in. You have healed us with your love. You have inspired us with your witness. Just by being faithful you have changed our lives. You are the answer to one of our prayers. Someone's second chance. Thank you. From us all.

January 24

We live in an age of extreme religion. Extreme escape or extreme control, but still extreme in the appeal of instant answers. For some to find the way out, the escape pod of bliss, the Om-ing of reality, becomes a privileged pastime. For many the claim of absolute law, the litmus test of the holy, becomes a blind obsession. To stand the ground of reason, to be both peace and action, to seek inner truth to engage outer need, to let go in order to have, these are skills of balance, the axis of witness on which religion will tip the world, toward compassion or confusion.

January 25

What will they say? Those future citizens of this blue pearl, for whom we are as distant on time's thread as the priests of Karnak, when all our monuments are stones and our voices but whispers. Will they say we were great for our faith in numbers: for treasure stored, for converts won, for points scored in debates long forgotten? Or will they stand amid our ruin and say that once on Earth a faith shone bright, a love beyond all measure, that transcended time with a message of peace, that birthed their world into hope, and honored the God of Ages? What they say then is what we do now.

January 26

O God, I pray today for all in silent struggle. For those who are webbed-in by addiction, for the ones who sit in quiet depression, for the carriers of chronic pain, for the person shut-in by frail experience. Let this prayer reach them as a source of strength. Break the tangles of dependence, lift away the shadows, comfort the bone deep hurt, bring joy to the door of the lonely. Into the silence let this word sail as if skimming beneath a running wind over the broad backed water, sparkling with health to shower the one in need in the sunlight of your great love.

January 27

Here is a word to the young woman or man who seeks to live the sacred life, to walk the way of faith. I call on all the rest of us to turn and show you our respect: your voice to hear, your truth to heed, your struggle to embrace. Forgive us if we seem slow to move, slow to understand. We do not know all you face, all you wake up to each day, but we can learn when we listen and be beside you when needed. You are the messengers of transformation, the ones who carry the weight of change. You are the pride of all those who have gone before, the young disciples who dare the dark to bring new light alive.

January 29

The promise of place. How often we feel out of place. We doubt the place we are. The young feel in an alien world, the old dread being sent away. The troubled home a home no more, the job a daily grind. The church a cold embrace, the bedroom an outpost beside an empty sea. Each life has known the moment when place becomes the fear of being alone. In these times, remind us God, that you have prepared a place, that where you are, we may also be. And since you are in every place, this place is where we may abide with thee.

January 30

You know you need to hit the refresh button for your faith when: you frown more than you smile; you worry more about sexuality than about the fate of dolphins; your last prayer had something to do with being found out; you can identify which denominations God likes; you put more money on a race than in a plate; you find nothing funny about the Bible; you actually believe you are in charge; you would rather talk to someone about being saved than give them something to eat; you think more about sin than about love.

January 31

We are all travelers, exploring the span of our lives, as though it was a foreign land, a map made real, both origin and destination. Like all travelers we find the journey sometimes tedious, irritating and uncomfortable. Too many strangers, too many crowds, waiting in lines, queuing up to see the same tired wonders. But then the unexpected happens, the flash of new awakening, the moment of serene rest, the odd feeling we have passed this way before. We are only tourists to our own time, until we open our eyes, to find the home we left behind, a surprise undiscovered.

FEBRUARY

February 1

Ihear many people say they are not religious but spiritual, that they do not like organized religion. That sounds good to me. I have been going to church for sixty years and I have never thought of myself as religious. It sounds too formal. My spiritual self wears blue jeans and has too many questions to ever get organized. I prefer a disorganized democracy of faith where other spiritual seekers can think for themselves. So if you are not very religious, and have a spiritual story to share, I hope to see you in church one day. Believe me, you will be among friends.

February 2

Patience is not so much a gift as a skill. It does not come unbidden, as though it were foreign to our nature, as though anger was our being, but rather it grows through practice, a steady art, made stronger by being so often tested. There are few disciplines as important. Few tools of the spiritual life more effective. Patient in our own struggle, patient in the need of others. Patient in our waiting, patient in our doing, patient in our receiving. Patience is how we learn. Patience how we become grace. Patience the peace of God embodied.

February 3

A man was once told to give away all he owned if he was to enter the realm of God. That should help us consider what we truly own. We do not own our possessions for they will stay when we will go. We do not own our children. We do not own our lives. We do not own the Earth around us, the sky above, or the waters of the sea. We do not own the truth even if we pretend otherwise. We are at the least only caretakers, at the best faithful stewards. Emptied of all we grasp to own, free of the need to control, we inherit everything that is, all there ever will be.

February 5

The peace which passes understanding is the peace that defies our logic. With lives under siege from a dozen directions, troubles too many to count, and bodies that seem to betray us when we need them most, we should be frantic, minds scattered like leaves before the wind. But a single still point of the Spirit, a grace serene and unmoving, calms the inner sea, breathes easy within the storm. God give you peace. Beyond all reason, despite all evidence, God give you peace. The peace that understands only you. The peace of a prayer answered before it was ever spoken.

February 6

To listen, to hear, to receive, even when the sounds are foreign. To think, to consider, to seek, even when the thoughts are new. To speak, to share, to offer, even when the ideas are risky. These three skills are the toolbox of faith. How well we use them determines how well we grow in understanding, build community, make our witness in the world. Spiritual life is not a flight from the real, but the real given wings to fly. With the simple tools God gave us, we craft our sacred space. We hear the other, we learn change, we speak healing to repair a broken world.

February 7

I am amazed at the power of the kind word, the pinpoint of grace. Like many seekers I have waded through volumes of wise words, streaming out from spiritual sources I imagine must be deep wells of knowledge. But have they shaped me more than the single word of love, of recognition, of comfort, spoken just when I needed it most? We all are sages of the kind word, the holy word of simple love and caring. No great torrent of great thoughts, but just a cup of water. When we speak what we can, as humble as it may be, we lift a soul to find its light, and set it flying free.

February 8

Do we love those nearest to us because they say what we want to hear or because they say what we need to hear? Agreement alone is not the measure of affection. Conformity is not the energy behind a working mind. A community that seeks to shout down opposition is soon silenced by its own inbred opinion. God did not come to smother the human spirit with the pillow peace of single thought obedience, but set that spirit afire with voices diverse and even divided. In so far as we learn to respect difference, we learn to become all our intellect can imagine.

February 9

Here is a key, an unlocking prayer, shaped to a single purpose. With clear intent I see it before me, a tool of sacred power. With this prayer what binds another, what shuts them in, what holds them fettered can be opened. Please God, let it be so. Let this prayer release one captive. Let it have authority over prison pain, addiction's chain, the dark closet of lonely memory. I cannot name the cage, but I can see the key. Send it through your grace, send it unseen, but soon felt, to unlock the life of another. Let it do for them what once it did for me.

February 10

I pray for all my sisters and brothers who live in lands without freedom. Those who dwell beneath the tyrant's shadow, whose lives are constricted by fear of their own neighbors, who suffer the blind brutality of petty power. I pray for them when they rise up and suffer even more for doing so. Caught in silence or civil war, pawns of global gamers who pass for wise leaders, I pray for their safety, for justice and for peace. Give them the right to live as they would choose, to pray as they please. Give them courage in this dark day and hope for their bright tomorrow.

February 12

We walk on water. As a child I did not understand and took the story for magic. But now I see that the boat is the illusion and the truth is waves beneath my feet. I do not know where my next step will take me. I have no certain ground that life will guarantee. With the weight of pride in mind, stones of judgment in hand, heart heavy in anger: I could so easily sink into the dark. But if I trust, if I forgive, if I love as I am loved, then my soul stands feather light, no matter the path I take. We walk on water every day. The challenge is to reach the shore.

February 13

You have been day dreaming again. Please don't be embarrassed. No apology needed. I believe when our Teacher went off alone to a lonely place to pray it was not always an intense focus kept, but often a dreamy wandering, a drifting mind on a still sea, carried by currents of imagination. God's vision is not a graph, the grand plan to fulfill, but often a sketch, a reality half seen through the shimmering sunlight, a playful world within. Dream on. You do not follow the Teacher in a stern march to reach a holy quota, but share a quiet moment day dreaming a different tomorrow.

February 14

When my time comes to hear applause let me listen with humility. When my time comes to admit mistakes let me do so with honesty. When I am to speak let it be truth as best I know it, when silent then attentive to what I may learn. When I receive let it be with thanks, when I give let me give with joy. When I must wait to wait in patience, when I must choose then choose most wisely. When my time comes to carry pain let me do so uncomplaining, when doing justice then with courage unfailing, and when leaving this life with peace my soul embracing.

February 15

Beware the drought to come. I ask all faithful eyes to watch thin clouds that feed thin streams while lakes draw back and rivers cease their race to a dying sea. Our gleaming towers are built on sand. Six billion dry throats will cry for the drink that runs down treeless hills to carry their life away. We are the people of water, it is our sacred story. Let us act now to guide our world to a place of peaceful sharing. Look up, people of God, for the drought to come will wither hearts of their compassion and make a desert of our dreams if we stand silent before the banks of the Jordan.

February 16

I dreamed last night I walked bright hills, beneath a perfect sky, surrounded by scores of children, who laughed at all I said. Innocent, pure, sparkling laughter, the joy of simple joy, a sound so healing it made meadows beneath our feet and set the birds to dancing. It is that wakening echo that I now send to you. I pray that memory to life, before it gets lost in daily cares, to weave itself through time and space, coming to rest around you, a ribbon of sound distant but clear, so clear you will hear it throughout this day. Be blessed by this echo, innocent beneath a perfect sky.

February 17

Feel the fire within. You were but cold dust until the hot breath of God set your soul to flame. Creation is energy. All the stars burn to bring life, their heat the hand of God, melting cold space to shape and shape again what makes life spring from rocks, beauty born from frozen form, movement warm and growing. You are the child of passion. That first spark glows deep within you. Name what stirs your blood, quickens your mind, frees your spirit to sing. Name the fire within and feel the touch of the God who made you.

February 19

How do we know what to believe, if we have climbed the mount of the transfiguration? The cloud descends to fog what was once bright vision. The compass spins with no clear spiritual direction. When you feel lost in the mist on the mountain do not be afraid, be still. Listen. There is a voice in that mist meant only for you. It calls you to see with the eyes of trust for only in trust can you walk the higher ground. The path is far from easy for those who would be made new. If you would be transformed you would know that what you do not see is what reveals the most about you.

February 20

Have you ever come home to find yourself waiting? So much of our outward lives are but jackets hanging by the door. We put them on, we wear our roles, we walk among the well-dressed. The private part we leave behind, by a window sitting. It is to that silent soul that God would pay a call. A quiet talk, a listening time, a word of truth shared between friends, while all the world clamors by, unknowing of the grace within your walls. Even while you do what must be done, God is doing what you need. You never sit alone when prayer is your companion.

February 21

When I cannot be there by your side, knowing that you need me, I leave this prayer in my place, until I am able to return. In our minds we draw clear lines of distance and imagine them to be real. But in our hearts there are no lines but only circles to enclose us. Through God's grace there is no space between you and me. I hold you still close to me every waking moment. And when you sleep I never leave, for in your dreams I am there, just as you are with me. Let my love for you be by your side all the long hours through until time passes by and we embrace once again.

February 22

In the interest of transparency, let me make my political agenda clear: heal the sick, cherish the children, honor the widow and the orphans. Judge no other person for how God made them. Make sure everyone gets something to eat. Build bridges of peace. Forgive others repeatedly but insist on always speaking the truth. Speak that truth to power. Turn over the tables of the money changers. Do not forbid others who pray differently. Define leaders as those who serve not those who talk. Pay attention to the Earth as a garden. Share love, not fear.

February 23

If I had walked with the first disciples and heard every word that was spoken, would the message have been perfectly clear to me? It was not so for them. They argued. They questioned. They denied. Even standing next to light, they still saw in shadow. Only in the living did they learn. Faith is not a truth to be recited, but an experience to be shared. If the Word is alive it lives in each of us, challenging us to grow. The message is not once given never to be doubted, but offered freely countless times in every moment when we have the choice to love and make that choice together.

F e b r u a r y   2 4

There you are with that mirror again. I should be used to it by now, but I'm not. Every Lent I come to you, O God, wanting your instant affirmation. Thinking you will be the god I thought I'd tamed. But in the quiet of your room, with never a word of condemnation, you hold up that mirror. I will not say what I see for the seeing needs no language. I will not deny the image nor question the reason for truth. Let the clock on the mantel be sound enough for what passes between us. Your warm embrace when I leave all the promise I need.

F e b r u a r y   2 6

In this political year I am announcing a new animal rights campaign: save the scapegoats. There are so many now, wandering innocent through our landscape. I see them almost everywhere. In fact, they look a lot like you and me. So I know they must all be God's creatures, with the same hopes, the same needs as us. I believe we should build a shelter where they can be safe from harm. A refuge where they can live in peace and not be targets for extinction. I even have a name for my scapegoat sanctuary: we can call it America.

February 27

I pray a holy season for you, a season of answered prayer. I know there must be a longing in your heart, a hope you carry close. It may be a sudden change, a deep desire, even an older wish made long years ago by a well of memory you believe may have gone dry. I will turn my own spirit toward you. I will join you in the stillness or the sorrow. I will lift my voice beside you. I will be the echo of your call. And while we wait together, to hear the reply, to see the result, I will share this season with you, the season of your answered prayer.

February 28

When the lights go out and the church is still does Mary ever come down to sit on her pedestal, rest her feet, warm her hands by the candle flame? Would we let her if she could? I think we do no kindness to our saints by making them stand at attention. Reverence does not require rigidity. I prefer that they live among us, unseen but never unknown, as human as you or I, fragile flesh not made of stone. The wonder of holy people is not that they were perfect, but flawed as they were they were remembered for doing more right than wrong.

February 29

Did the minds behind the hands that raised Stonehenge imagine their reality would go on forever? Did the citizens of Sumer or Chichen Itza or Harrppa believe theirs was the way the world would stay? Each culture claims its moment. Each age assumes reality. But even the foreheads of nations are marked with the ashes of time. Do not despair, Ozymandias, for loss of the ephemeral. Even the Pleiades may be passing, but the God who spins the seasons and knits the threads of time will offer a gift eternal to let love the last Word be.

MARCH

M a r c h   1

Beware the Ides of March, Caesars walk among us. Our history tells us of how so often the few can rule the many. Narcotic power sits on thrones draped in many flags. Each claims the right to design destiny for the people who must serve and suffer. Terror guards the palace, fear invades the temple, war collects the taxes. We do not escape this truth with appeasement or denial. What happens far away happens close to home. Stand up good citizens of faith, from every race and religion, join in a single prayer that peace and justice may prevail.

M a r c h   2

I pray the curtain parted, if only enough to let shine in a single ray of light. There are questions we all have carried, the cargo of our conscience, for years without an answer. Family matters dark and tangled, friendships complex in nature, mistakes made and chances missed, the source of the Nile for our sorrows. As a veteran of many vigils I do not expect all to be revealed. Not now. But I will claim an insight. I will pray a discovery. May God grant you a glimpse, a thread of truth to follow, that curious hope may guide you, to the answer you seek the most.

March 4

Grief comes, a quiet stranger, to stand before our door. How unwelcome a guest, and yet how familiar. We may sit with grief for hours, talking of our loss, or sit in silence long passing, the loss a loss for words. Grief resides in many homes today, and it is for those homes I pray. May the love of God be present while grief must abide. May the comfort of the Spirit remain ever by your side. May the peace of God be with you until grief takes its leave, only a shadow left behind, in the light of a promise eternal, from which we never depart.

March 5

Let this prayer be a string on your finger, a reminder when you need it most, that Someone is watching over you. How easy it is to turn a corner and discover we are alone. At odds with the one we love, anxious about the rent, struggling with work, waiting for the doctor to call: how quickly we are thrown into the emptiness that waits just beyond our walls. Keep this prayer for such a day. You are not alone in life. You are not abandoned. The string on your finger is a beacon, a signal into the silence. It calls love to find you, hope around the corner, when you need it most.

March 6

I dreamed that all the religions fell silent. We all awoke one day to a world where no priest could preach, no mullah proclaim, no rabbi teach, no guru say a word. Our books were gone, our effort to write only a blank page. We knew the faith of each one, but could learn only by observation. We could speak of other things, but in matters of belief we were stilled. The world became a witness. There is no stronger argument for faith than the life you lead. If others do not see God in what you do, they will not hear it in what you say.

March 7

Forgive them for they know not what they do or forgive them because they do. Most of the things I have done that would bring me to seek forgiveness were not done through ignorance or intent, but by that subtle sin of suspended awareness, the half-closed eyes of the mind, the automated art of anger. Forgive me, God, for the vanity of my pretense: that I did not know what I knew and imagined you would not notice. My practiced deception convicts my heart of crimes against my conscience. Forgive me for trying to hide between the shadows of ignorance and knowing.

March 8

Evangelism is what we like to talk about but not do. Stewardship is what we do but don't like to talk about. Sermons are what we say we believe. Outreach is what we believe we say. Hymns are what we pray when we sing. Budgets are what we pray when we plan. Liturgy is how we act when we are being the church. Coffee hour is how we act when we are the church. Sunday school is where our kids go to play and sometimes quarrel. Conventions are where our adults go to do the same thing. Clergy are laity doing a saintly job. Laity are people doing all the other jobs because they are saints already.

March 9

I pray for what troubles you, that center point of shadow that hides within your heart. It may be as new as this morning or as old as a memory. It may be as heavy as the weight of guilt or as light as the cloud that passes before the moon. But it is there. It is always there. I turn my spirit toward you. With prayerful purpose I turn my mind to search you out, across all distance and through the clutter of restless time. Nothing will separate us. Nothing will keep my prayer from you. God's grace touch you now, free you now, from what troubles you, a burden you carry no more.

M a r c h 1 1

W hat promise do you believe? Each election year is a civic Lent when we will reflect deeply on what we believe. We will weigh what we hear against what we see. The scales of truth will hang on a thread of promise. The answer a vote of hope. Already the call to conscience sounds across the electronic sea. It will only grow louder until shouts of promise fill the air and political passion sweeps the faithful forward. Remember this word when that time comes, be mindful of its message. The future hides in the past: what is done determines what is to come.

M a r c h 1 2

W here does passion go as time carries us through the slip-stream years? Is it lost along the way, jolted from us by some great disappointment, or does it simply drift away, bright leaves made brittle, drifting on an autumn wind? Age negotiates our dreams and barters our experience. Compromise accommodates need at the cost of vision. Do not go gentle into that good night, but hold your passion precious. What you once saw, what you once felt, is the spark to light a distant fire, out there, where cold children wait for your arrival.

March 13

Last night I heard a mother praying, praying in words I could not decipher, but with a meaning clear. She was praying her child would survive the war. She was pleading safety and protection. She was praying in Damascus, in Kabul and the Gaza Strip. She was praying in Omaha, in Chicago and Virginia Beach. She was praying in a dozen languages, but her words were all the same. Let the madness end. Let the children live. Let the peace of God prevail. Today I will pray with her. I hope she hears me, knowing she is not alone, my voice unfamiliar, but with a meaning clear.

March 14

God's grace is not an object but an energy. It is not a thing once given, as if it were a reward, but a force of transformation that alters the fabric of the finite. It moves. It bends and shapes and flows. Like liquid love it wraps around obstacles firmly set and renews them with the chemistry of change. Faith is how we draw grace toward us. Hope is how we focus its power. Love is how we release it into life. When these three are in motion, the energy becomes tangible. Prayer is the catalyst. Mission the action of grace: God's gift at work in the world.

March 15

Do not be afraid. There is a message for every household of faith to share. When doom and gloom are running for office, and the streaming news is a flood of woe, when the next budget cut could be you or me, and the search for answers is a search for who to blame: fear seems like safety and control the only chance. Into this suspicious time let our subversion be at work. Hope not fear, peace not war, love not hate, give not take, a chant simple but insistent, a light that shines in shadow, a place to take a stand when all the sands seem shifting.

March 16

Greater minds than mine are at work on how to save the church. Experts in demographics, organizational gurus, masters of mission strategy: they gather with those in power to plan the path to promise. I pray them well. I have no secret formula to fill our phantom pews, but only an experience for what worth it may share. To grow a church preach from the heart, work for the poor, welcome the stranger, embrace the Spirit. Laugh more than cry. Fail more than wait. Give more than keep. Be unexpected love and trust the becoming to God.

March 18

I looked and saw the Spirit glide in on widespread wings, Her blessings falling like showers of light, Her movement a song whose very sound brought healing to all who heard it. I watched Her hand pass over many who slept in sorrow, knowing they would soon awake to discover misplaced hope, awake to answered prayers, awake to strength renewed. I felt Her passing through the night, beneath the shawl of stars, Her great love left for all to see, in the dawn to come.

March 19

What authority has been given to you? Consider your answer well for it may be different than you think. Not the generic ability to resist an evil or the task of a job description, but the inner light of a gift, placed by purpose in your soul, an awareness deep grown through time, a Word from the source of words, entrusted into your care. We each have an authority given to us. We each have a calling. Part mission, part mystery, a sacred quest to discover, a reason for being found in the fulfilling. Name the path and you see the destination.

March 20

I learned a valuable lesson yesterday from a coffee shop waitress who was tired and let it show. She did not greet me with a corporate smile but showed me where to sit like someone who was over worked or worried or both. She gave me an excuse to pay her back with attitude and no tip left on the table. But instead I smiled and wished her well until the mask fell away. Tired feet and a long day soothed by a moment of caring. She was laughing as I left, the next customer warmly greeted. Our minimum wage should be simple kindness shared at every table.

March 21

I write these words each morning, alone in a pool of light, while prayer candles are flickering, my world still sleeping, the silence an invitation, the memories and the meaning, a truth waiting for dawn to find it. We are not random strangers, you and I, skimming the online stream, but characters in a shared story, brought together on these screens to see what we were meant to see. Between the writing and the reading a mystery entwines us both: you knew what I would say before I found words to speak it.

March 22

What is truth? Soon we will hear Pilate's question again, echoing through the sacred drama of long ago, echoing still on all the uneasy borders of religion. For some the answer is a fortress, for some a weapon, for some a marketplace. The search for this single prize has graced our history with noble lives whose love inspires us still. It has caused deep suffering and laid waste the lives of many. What is truth? Come reverently to the question. Do not pull the answer like a trigger. The truth you live is as close to holy power as you may ever come.

March 23

I have tasted God in fresh farm corn and creamery butter eaten by a roadside stand with slippery fingers and smiles. I have smelled God in the cinnamon air of wood smoke drifting on an autumn breeze. I have touched God on the nestling skin of a sleeping infant held close to share my heartbeat. I have seen God walking away into a coastal sunset turning the fiery water to green beneath purple streamers. This body of mine is not some poor shell to house the divine seed until it ripens, but the many senses God gave to help me understand what my mind can never comprehend.

March 25

Last night I sat beneath a sliver of a moon, doing nothing more important than talking to someone I love, while the city around me went about its business of being. An evening so unremarkable it lulled me away from care and left me drifting in the rare place we call contentment. The peace of God rises up when we least expect it. It materializes out of the thin air where the space between here and heaven allows us to pass from the complex world we create to the simple shores of serenity. The dream becomes the awakening.

March 26

If I were bold enough to proclaim a healing, would you be bold enough to believe me? I work no miracle more than you. I have no special power to offer. But I do know that when we bring our love to bear, when we seek mercy, when we summon comfort from the far reaches of hope, something happens. Take my prayer as your own. Feel our words as one. Let this healing be our soul shared certainty, our fixed point of faith. Be bold not because you expect magic, but because like me you have been witness to a wholeness that no broken body can deny.

M a r c h   2 7

We see the cracks once more, the deep divides between our people, color-coded distrust, acted out on dark nights, spilling over into streets of rage. The loss of any life is a sorrow, the loss of justice a crime. God help us to overcome the myth of race, the fear of one another, the hurts we inflict for no reason. Teach us to stand together in respect for human dignity. Let our kinship become a pledge no hate can subvert. Remind us that in your eyes we are all children, each unique in how we live, but all loved just the same, a seamless love unbroken.

M a r c h   2 8

Some hurts are splinters in the soul, memories embedded, a sliver of pain that has worked itself under the skin. We can carry them with us for years. The problem is that they rarely work themselves out. Over time they can get infected. Bitterness is their by-product. An inability to forgive their symptom. It is never easy to take a soul splinter out. We flinch at the idea of re-visiting something we would as soon forget. But with holy patience, spiritual courage, and the steady hand of the Spirit, we can slowly release their injury and be free of their wound.

March 29

The hour will come, the time of my passing. I do not know when or how. I do not know if I will be surprised or relieved or aware. I only know that I will one day stand with my back to what has been and my face toward what I will discover. When that moment arrives I pray a simple passing prayer: receive me as I am, O God, as trusting in your kindness as when I first breathed the breath you gave me. Forgive my faults, reveal my learnings, bless those I leave behind. Let my love redeem what is past and welcome what is to come.

March 30

I pray for leadership in the church, for those who sit in convention, for the one who will sit on a throne. I pray with no agenda, for we have agendas enough to fill a cathedral, and practitioners of partisan piety in abundance. I pray for honest hearts, clear minds and pure spirits. I pray renewal. I pray courage. I pray the power of Spirit, a fresh wind of hope and change. I pray the Word to speak to still the sounds of fear. I pray justice for each and all, I pray the poor to stand tall. I pray the church takes back the church. I pray the moment come.

APRIL

A p r i l   1

So what are you welcoming into your life these days? Every morning the love of God comes to us, seeking to enter into our gates. God arrives humbly, not to take control, but to take our side, to be a source of support, a very present help in time of trouble. If you are like me, you can often take that for granted. You can forget to leave the fortress walls to find the peace outside. But there are few things more worthy of thanksgiving then the knowledge that an everlasting compassion is always waiting to be welcomed into our lives.

A p r i l   2

Today I will renew my vows as a priest. It has made me think how important a thing it is to promise. And yet, in this age, how often a pledge is made as though it had an expiration date stamped on its side. Someone once said our character can be measured by our ability to make a promise and keep it. Our word is our bond. It may seem old-fashioned and outdated, but I still want to live by those words. I want to be as good as my word. I pray God will hear my vow, and even more, help me to keep it.

April 3

Praying beside a bed in an ICU yesterday I saw a man open his eyes to the world he should have left behind. He was the Easter story brought to life for one very over-joyed family. The mercy of God accepts no constraints, not even death. No matter how difficult your life may be, it is still life, that precious thread of breath that God may use as a lifeline to pull you to a second chance. Resurrection is neither myth nor miracle, but the work God performs around us each day. Open your eyes. See the world as life to which you were born to belong.

April 4

You are a good, kind and caring person who deserves all the love you ever receive. No, don't shake your head. I know that automatic switch. It comes from the hand of memory. Just let these words rest before you. Let them rest lightly on your heart. How rare the simple language of recognition, the steady gaze of gentle blessing, seeing past your past to know you. You are a good, kind and caring person who deserves all the love you ever receive. That is how God thinks of you. That is how I think too.

A p r i l 5

Tonight in many churches we will perform the symbolic act of foot washing. In our time it demonstrates the ideal of humble service to others. But it makes me think of another truth, sometimes overlooked. In ancient days it was women, both servants and free, who did most of the washing. They washed the feet of men. The scandal of the Messiah who would do the work of women should not be lost on us. The symbol is not humility, but equality, a vision still as distant for us in this age as it was for those sisters of long ago whose place was on bended knee.

A p r i l 6

Life begins in the tomb. Vision is born of darkness. Hope emerges from despair. Since time first played the music that set the human mind to dance, we have watched the waltz of yin and yang, across the floor of heaven. No light without dark, no life without death. The pattern is not the problem. It is the heart that is to blame. For no change occurs without feeling, that pain that turns the balance of creation to poetry, when what we see so clearly is obscured by the tears we cannot avoid, a child seeing the flower wither, an elder bidding the sun good-bye.

April 8

He is risen. He is risen in the nursing home, in county jail and the local bar. He is risen in the undocumented home, the penthouse and the trailer. He is risen in Syria and Cairo, in LA and NYC, in villages without a name. He is risen in the broken heart, the troubled mind, the soul hiding beneath the bridge. He is risen in the nightshift nurse, the boy soldier, the homeless man under the cardboard cathedral. He is risen in the war room, the boardroom, the room without windows. He is risen in you and me, in our children, in those who were and those about to be.

April 9

God bless the mystics among us, the theological day dreamers, the untamed minds that cannot stop wondering why. Never let us become prisoners of the pragmatic, O God, bean counting the church into a definition. Let us be nomads of imagination, a small tribe in a great land, discovering you around every unexpected corner. Our faith is best when not weighted by convention of culture, but questioning what constrains the human heart or denies the justice of the common spirit. Let us be like you, God, a wild grace whose love is without borders.

A p r i l   1 0

Here is an Easter prayer for those whose hope of resurrection is not so much to live forever as to simply live another day. The world is full of people who measure life with a sunrise. The soldier at war, the child on life support, the addict looking for a fix, the many who wake up hungry. Eternal life is a distant goal when daily life is an end in itself. My own salvation has no joy if in rising I leave others behind. Take my part of Easter's light, dear God, and share it with those in shadow. Let me wait for your promise until they can claim it with me.

A p r i l   1 1

Jesus doing the dishes, Moses mowing the lawn. Buddha running the vacuum, Mary cleaning the bathtub. When I was young I thought if I attained a spiritual life I would think great thoughts, say nice things, do good. While some of that may be true, I have learned it is truth that still needs to make its own bed. So here is to all of you who like me have your head in heaven and your hand on a mop. The holy life is not always a mountain top experience, but an experience of a mountain of pots and pans. God bless the gurus who take out the garbage. You know who you are.

April 12

Good news. Good news we proclaim on this streaming river that bears so many stories of sorrow. Good news we cry into dark winds that scatter the hope of many. Good news we whisper into the ear of the one who feels alone. Good news we are when standing silent before the powers who deny justice. Good news we embody when hate seeks to steal the gift of love. Good news we live in the midst of death. Good news we pass to children. Good news we wrap around our elders. Good news we were born to be. Good news our final blessing.

April 13

We live in an uneasy age, when doubt urges greed to claim what it can, and confidence fades as the old temples go unattended. Public leaders walk backwards, showing us what was as though the past is what we should become. Distraction is big business. Information outsells wisdom. Technology the magic on which we rely. You and I were born to this time, though we feel no part of it. We are here to witness to the quiet prophecy of reason, the healing of sharing, the hope that does not fear the future. We are stewards of a faith that is not anxious, peace when peace is hard to find.

April 15

May the peace of God be with you. I do not know what you face. I do not know what you have been through or what awaits you still. But I do know that your heart hopes for strength, your mind seeks for answers, your soul longs for the companionship that only faithful friends can offer. May God's strong arm hold you up. May God's wisdom guide you. May God's good people come to stand beside you. Take this prayer with you. Let it rest quietly in your spirit, come what may. Let it be what you most need it to be: the peace of God within you.

April 16

Dream on, all of you who like to turn the gray of your world into a spray of color, sitting quietly in your chair, with your mind inventing places just on the far side of imagination. We should not lose our love of pretend as we grow older, but be all the better at it for the years we have invested in reality. The spirit that is not playful is the spirit that has lost its wings. So dream on serious scholars, reliable parents, hardworking pastors. Let your slight smile confuse those around you as inside you dance to music we have never heard and watch sunsets on worlds of wonder.

A p r i l 1 7

G reat is the courage of the women and men who struggle to make a living. It is not easy to face another day when that day means long hours for little pay. It is not easy to hold a family together when your arms are tired from lifting the weight of hard work. These brave souls deserve our respect. They are worthy of every prayer. Bring them the justice they have earned, God, bring them the hope of their deepest dream. Let them see light at the end of their long tunnel, the light of the One who once spoke to them on a hillside with baskets of bread over-flowing.

A p r i l 1 8

S ilence. I have come to value silence. I live in a world sound soaked, where every electronic device joins the chorus, as though talking could drown the empty spaces, the flood of noise a reassurance that we really do have something to say. We are a babbling ball, broadcasting our chatter into the multiverse that surrounds us, never noticing the silence in which we float. I do not think we hear God's word best when talking at the same time. Let the sermon be stillness, the lecture unspoken meditation, that others may hear more clearly the wisdom that waits within.

April 19

This is how they will know us, that we do the work of God. Each day we clock in to take our part in making life worth living. Some turn to great tasks, to speak for justice and stand against the ruin of Earth. Some perform the healing art of caring for those in need. Some do the countless small jobs of sharing kind words, holding hands, cleaning away the clutter that the path ahead is clear. Some pray. Some study. Some teach. Some sing. Some simply love their family. In all we do, we take our part, the work of God, to make life worth living. This is how they know us.

April 20

There is a heaven. I know this beyond doubting for I have been there. There is a second life to come. I believe this without question for I have experienced it. Heaven is when you are where you most want to be, doing what you want to do, with the ones you love. The second life comes to us in many ways. After addiction, after cancer, after grief, after betrayal: there are many after-lives we have survived to live again. I do not know if I should expect wings and a harp, but I will settle for these heavens and second chances. And be grateful to God forever.

April 22

Compromise. I had to make a compromise. I had to balance what I believed against what someone else needed. How often we prefer to imagine our role in faith to be without ambiguity. We are heroic statues in public parks without the need to move. But in fact it is often in compromise that we see the wheels of mission turn. Love would be stillborn if we never found the humility to seek a balance. Truth is not always discovered. It is also negotiated. God give us the skill of compromise: the wisdom to seek you not only on mountain tops but on common ground.

April 23

Today I will conjure love from the empty air. I will call it out from thin places where people walk without breathing, from dark places where they stumble without seeing. I will find love in those I do not like and let love appear in the faces I avoid. I will make room for love in my life even if I feel overcrowded with worry. I will offer love without restraint even if I have not received love in return. I will dance with love in innocent pleasure. I will sing love as though my voice were a new discovery. Today I will be the love God made me be when God called me from the empty air.

April 24

It is not easy to live out here, here in the rift valley, between the great forces of nothing and all. No wonder so few want to dare it. It is far safer to stand on the high ground of exclusion, claiming absolutes in every direction. It is easier to be on the calm heights of uncaring, where no faith is required to watch the stars. The church built on the fault lines of fear seems a folly to those already afraid, but to the disciples of the One whose arms are widespread, whose love knows no margins, whose justice no bounds, it is the only place to be.

April 25

I am not sure what is around the next corner of your life, but I will walk that way with you if you like. I will keep you company in prayer until we both see what life has in store for us. And as we walk I will remind you that we are both veterans of many twists and turns. We have the experience to face change, the wisdom to think it through, the courage to do what must be done, the faith to know there is love on the other side. We may not know what is coming, but we do know that we are not alone. We can walk together. We can walk with God by our side.

April 26

We live in an age that equates religion with fear. With violence, intolerance and conflict. We expect that religious people will hold extreme views and demand conformity with their way of thinking. We are afraid to talk about religious things. We step lightly to avoid the mine field. The price we pay is our silence. We have been cut off from one another. We must reclaim religion from extremism. We must learn again how to speak of faith without cringing. We must show others how to share faith with open minds, kind hearts and a desire to learn. We must speak to listen.

April 27

We are always becoming what we will be. Each day, each moment, each choice is a movement of the sculptor's hand. We mold the clay from which God raised us, shaping ourselves into the form of our own lives. We cannot blame others if the image is not to our liking, for even if we are damaged, we are capable of change. We are clay, not stone. Like any artist we are not perfect in our craft and some days may be harder than others. But in the end, we become what we will be by the attention we give to the art that is our life. The rest is grace.

April 29

May the peace that passes understanding surround you with calm assurance. May the wisdom that overcomes doubt guide you to an answer. May the hope that transcends every fear strengthen you in spirit. May the love that lives in spite of loss keep you safe in its embrace. Be blessed today. Be blessed in all you do. Be blessed by those who stand beside you, by those far away, by those you hold in memory. Be blessed by the prayer you never hear, but that speaks your name. Be blessed by these words as they carry the Word to find your faith unfailing.

April 30

When did it start for you? When did spiritual awareness first break the surface of your mind? For some of us it came early, for others only after a long journey. For some in a flash, for others in a series unfolding. We are explorers of discovery. We find the holy in unexpected places, at different ages, within our own story. We find it in ways unique and in long loved tradition. God is scattered like diamonds, like dew dust, like an ancient city still proud beneath the clasp of jungle. When did it start for you? When did mystery claim your heart and wonder first know your name?

MAY

M a y   1

Hope is the match, prayer is the fire. If you know someone who needs a little help in getting a prayer life going, ask them if they ever hope for something. It's a safe bet that they do. And all the time. Humans are hopeful creatures. We are in an almost daily state of hope. We hope it won't rain. We hope we get better. We hope we win. Hope is a constant for us in our emotional matrix. Prayer is simply hope captured. Rather than a fleeting wish, through prayer hope becomes a focused intention. Prayer matures hope by allowing God to light a fire.

M a y   2

It will be ok. How simple those words are. How often I have used them. In all the times I have tried to offer comfort or care, to help, to share, to give some word that had meaning enough to reach a heart so badly broken, I have found that phrase weaving its common way among the language of my learning. Street corner theology. The blessing of the everyday. It will be ok. Our universal affirmation of a truth known before there were cathedrals. The instinct of our courage. The bond of our fragile strength. The first feeling of faith: it will be ok.

M a y   3

G reat ideas work best in humble ways. If we proclaim
universal love, how well do we greet the stranger at
coffee hour? If we announce justice, how do we practice
that ten blocks from the parish door? If we speak of
compassion, how does that translate to the elders and
children in our own congregation? The Sermon on the
Mount sounded great, but it was the love lived on the
ground that caused the poor to gather. Let us bring vision
down from distant heights until it becomes the truth seen
when doubt looks us in the eye.

M a y   4

S it still. Sit still anxious minds. Sit still racing hearts,
wagging tongues, flailing hands. Do not pace the
problem you seek to catch or wring the answer from
nervous fingers. The flash of temper will not burn the
solution from empty air. Blame will not assign the meaning
onto another. The way out is not through a frantic search
as if the soul were lost keys. Come sit by me. Sit still.
Breathe. Breathe until breathing is all there is, the calm air
of God's quiet morning. You do not need to move for God
to find you. Your salvation seeks you in stillness.

M a y   6

I got inspired the other day. No, not by deep thoughts or sacred visions, but by the desire to do some house work. Now that's a miracle. I picked up piles of papers, tossed the junk mail, swept the carpets, dusted the books, washed the windows. I even emptied out the refrigerator of any food that could be used as a science project. Now that the rooms around me sparkle, I think I will work on the rooms within. Take out the prejudice, toss the fear, dust off the hope, sweep my soul of all the cobwebs of envy. I will do my house work that I may be home to what is holy.

M a y   7

Here is a prayer for the hollow places, for the hollow people, for the emptiness inside. How often our lives are determined by the need to fill something within us, something stolen away when we were small, something that has long gone missing. So tender is this space we rarely speak of it in public, but shelter down in our souls to hold it hidden. It can make us brittle. It can make us rage or cry or fear. We can seek to fill it with power or pills, drink or drama, but wake more empty than before. Come good Spirit and give us the love that heals the hollow we know but never name.

May 8

Y ou are a child of innocence, born to wonder all your days. Do not believe it to be a gift that you lost somewhere along the way, as if the hurts you have done or that were done to you could steal its light from the center of your soul. Innocence is not the absence of pain, but the ability to face truth as an adult while still seeing with the eyes of a child. Innocence is hope. It is vision. It is love. God grant that each of us, for all the darkness we have endured, will always have the grace of innocence: the belief that what is to come will be better than what has been.

May 9

I went to a meeting last night, a gathering of church leaders, sitting through reports and minutes and budgets and planning. How easy it might be to dismiss the moment as only another of the same in a long line of meetings stretching out into my memory. How easy to smile at the humor we all have for the many meetings we have endured. But let me give credit where credit is due. Meetings are miracles. That human beings share time and thoughts and minds and meaning for no other reason than to do good: God bless the much maligned meeting.

May 10

Here is a prayer for every person who stood outside in the cold for the sake of conscience. For the lone voice speaking for those who have no voice, for the one who risks a place at the table so that others may join the feast. We are not called to be comfortable, but rather to challenge the comfort that hides injustice. If our discipleship has no cost, it has no value. Do not fear to speak up for what you believe is right. Fear the silence if you do not speak for in that silence we all will be lost.

May 11

Today I claim a jubilee for all who carry a burden in their heart. In the Bible days of old the Jubilee was a time when debts would be forgiven. What you owed was erased, the loan of all sorrow paid in joy. While I cannot proclaim my jubilee for a year, I can invite you to join me in it for a day. Live this day without regret. Live the freedom of redemption. Feel the lightness of life without guilt, the open air of a pure conscience. Walk with me the path of jubilee, the experience of a love whose forgiveness sets the soul to sing.

M a y   1 3

L et us stretch the arms of sentiment to embrace every
woman who lives the role of mother. She may have
children of her own. She may not. It does not matter. The
woman who is teacher, mentor, care-giver, Godmother,
aunt, or friend: all may come beneath our tent of blessing
today. For we raise the hymn of praise beyond the Hallmark
greeting to honor the depth of what women give, what
women share, what women are, all the world round. To
mother is to lead, a steady hand to hold all life, to birth the
hope of generations in a single female heart.

M a y   1 4

Y ou cannot catch the soul train if you are loaded down
with too much baggage. That train of hope runs the
rails of heaven on lightning wheels, it waits on no human
time and answers to no agenda but the call to board in love.
If you are carrying anger or pride, bitterness or envy, you
will need to drop that luggage and let your feet fly to reach
that step that leads you to glory. Let go of what weighs you
down, let go of what you think you need. An open heart is
your ticket. An open mind your place on the fast track to
freedom. Welcome aboard!

May 15

In each farewell there is a piece of eternity that passes between us. We stand awkward before the moment. Time to go. Time to embrace. To say, see you soon and thank you and travel safely. Then in turning to face the world without the ones we leave behind. Such small movements. So often repeated. But in each good-by, there is a reminder of who we are: alone save for the presence of those who care enough to cling to us in careless time, holding us with a promise to return, an echo of a divine promise, an embrace that turns the farewells of life into the eternity of love.

May 16

Take each hour God's grace offers as though it were a single jewel to be threaded on the necklace of time. Each hour made precious, a gift meant just for you, that takes the earthy edges of hard stone and polishes them to shine with the inner light of your own spirit. These hours then are not heavy footed time, marching thoughtless through shadows, but sparkling chances given to discover hints of heaven in every waking moment. Be alert to what you have received, be mindful of what you wear, all you ever need is in each hour, you value enough to care.

May 17

Good morning, silent friend, where ever you may be. I cast this prayer out for you, a single strand of words, twined around hope and healing, to bridge the distance between us, a simple gift to cling to, a reminder that we are not alone, we two among the many, we fellow travelers in spirit, walking the hard roads, but singing, still singing, in spite of it all. Be at peace today. Be comforted come what may. I will hold this thread of faith on my end, keeping you safe in prayer. You hold it on your end, until in the quiet hours you let loose this bond until another day.

May 18

Let me unfurl my sails and make for the open sea. I am not afraid to see the far horizon as my only course. I do not need the crowded land to be my only harbor. I will let the wind chase me over the waves, skimming beneath the cloudless sky, steering through the night by the stars I choose to follow. I will trust myself to be this free for I know that God accepts me just as I am, empowers me as I am made, and will share my joy as I dare to go as far as I can before I reach that distant shore where the light of an endless love will bring me safely home.

M a y   2 0

May God bless all those who seek to live together in love. May your house never seem too small for the two of you, even when you are arguing. May your challenges never seem too great to face together, or too easy to make your days dull. May laughter bind your wounds and embraces free your hearts. May patience keep you talking, humor keep you smiling, kindness keep you caring. May people always see in you the love they long to live, the peace they want to share. May you live in light. May your dream never end or your hope fade away. Be two in mind, but one in blessing.

M a y   2 1

Some predictions for your future! You will get older. You will have more troubles. You will have more joys. You will keep working on something you have been working on for years. You will make a discovery that you will think of as a breakthrough. You will wear sad days like a garland of faded flowers. You will dance in your heart for the good news you will hear. You will gain weight. You will lose. You will gain. You will say goodbye to old friends. You will meet a strange person. You will have bad luck. You will forget about "luck" and trust in God and do something simply amazing and wonderful.

M a y   2 2

I have felt the power of one of your prayers in my life. I have been on the receiving end of your compassion. I know how strong that river flows. So I take this moment to honor you, to thank you, for the prayers you offer so faithfully for so many and for so long. Your prayers have been blessings, cast out like seeds caught on a breeze, bringing life out of unexpected soil, and hope from the tipping point of faith. Please keep it up. Please keep using the gift you have to make the forgotten come to mind and the lost discover the way home. Keep praying.

M a y   2 3

Do not doubt the faith that brought you this far, do not doubt the hope that you still carry. I know that your journey has been a long one, with enough disappointments along the way to discourage a saint, but you trusted yourself to make this climb, you believed in who God made you, and you took the chance. Don't quit now. Don't turn away. The outcome may not go according to plan, but it will be a blessing. You did not come this long distance to miss the moment when you know the destination was worth the trip. Sometimes to have faith, you just keep moving.

M a y   2 4

Walk lightly toward the evening of your age, do not be in a hurry to reach the end of your path, but let your youth still glow in the shadows like a sunset that lingers on the horizon. Shine bright with wisdom, shine bright with faith. Let all of your experience count, the good and the bad, and all that drifted in-between the spaces of your life when you weren't looking. Use what you have learned. Let your breathing be for a purpose, a vision made from the leftover memory, the unorganized dream. Your age has meaning when given away to the games of children.

M a y   2 5

Right isn't easy. Not usually. Wrong is easy. Wrong is a franchise on every corner, a parking place right out front, a lay-away plan that lets you keep paying for years. Right is all up hill, a choice that costs more than it pays, a way to lose friends and influence people. Because of this reality, I am even more grateful to you that you choose to do the right thing. Thank you for that. I know it cannot have been easy. I know it has cost you. But you do the right thing. You make the right choice. You welcome when others would turn away.

M a y   2 7

May the flame of the Spirit burn brightly in the church today. May it dance and flicker and scorch and singe and get us to move. May it be just far enough out of our control to make us uneasy. May its light wake up the sleepy and its warmth comfort the ones who cannot find rest. May the Spirit speak through a thousand voices whose meaning is known to the stranger who sits in the far back corner for fear of being welcomed. May the house of God shine today, and every day, with the fire that first kissed us when we huddled in the darkness, the fire that still burns in hearts too holy to accept the cold.

M a y   2 8

It is a good day to pray for peace, this day when we go to the grave, to the silent places where soldiers sleep, to offer our respect for what they gave, and lift our whispers of hope against the need to ever ask such a price of any young life again. God give peace to the fallen, peace to the ones coming home, peace to those waiting for them. Let peace be the highest honor bestowed, peace the blessing bought, full paid by lives too soon ended, and peace the breeze beneath the trees, where bowed heads remember what broken hearts cannot forget.

May 29

I sat with one of our elders, talking through the night, imagining what our future might be, telling some of the old stories that make us new. What I did not understand my son translated, the sound of how our ancestors spoke, one generation weaving threads of language to bind a culture together. I grow each time I stop to listen. I learn each time I am present to my teachers. I return to my homeland, to the red earth where my people still sing, to hear what only they can tell me, to see the past through ancient eyes, to see who I am when I look into the mirror of my heart.

May 30

Good-bye. So long. See you later. I think we have so many ways of saying farewell because we don't like doing it. We try to discover just the right words that will make going our separate ways easier. But it is never easier. It always hurts. When the bonds have been true, warm and genuine as real friendships are, then the touch of grief that lingers before the good-bye is a fixed price, the one we pay for caring. It is not time we cannot control, but memory. Even as we leave, we take the memory with us, a small and precious cargo, made more so by our parting.

M a y   3 1

If you have not had a chance to come to know Mary yet, this might be a good day to begin. Many years ago I stumbled into her in an empty church on a day that could not assemble enough clouds to be as dark as I felt. Mary brought healing and hope back to life, slowly, and with infinite care. What she has done for me, she does for millions, for all who will turn to her and open their hearts. Often trivialized or ignored, the real Mary is a source of wisdom and strength. I hope you will find her today, waiting in a silent space for you, where you need her most.

JUNE

J u n e 1

An answer to your prayer is coming to you. It may not arrive exactly as you imagined, but you will recognize it when it happens. The pieces will fall together. The situation will change. Something unexpected will enter into the picture. At that moment, you will realize again one of the deepest truths of human faith: someone is listening when you pray. Someone hears you, cares for you, knows you. From that tiny seed of experience great religions grow. But they all begin when an answer is received to an appeal as ancient as time and a hope as new as now.

J u n e 3

Here is love when you need it most, love flowing out like a rush of water through dry land, love breaking down barriers, moving without ceasing into every corner of life, healing the hurt places and freeing the darkened mind, love dancing in the lonely rooms, painting the house with fresh color, turning the city into a garden before anyone has noticed. The love of God is a force. It moves. It reshapes. It creates. Stand in that energy and feel the power of holy love to carry you where you need to go. Just open your heart and fly.

June 4

So what are you and St. Jude working on now? They say he is the saint of lost causes, the faithful one who will never give up on what he believes. Sounds like you. I suspect you two have met. I am sure he understands why you continue to support a vision that only a few others seem to share. I hope he admires you as I do, admires you for not jumping on the bandwagon, but staying on the ground to help the ones who missed the parade. No cause is lost until we let it go. No person is lost until they refuse to be found. Tell Jude to wait, I will be right there.

June 5

I hear the rustle of wings around me. I hear the half-heard voices of angels speaking as they gather, the faint impression of form moving like smoke against the first light of morning. I feel the pulse of energy from the Spirit as She raises Her wings to fly. I know that all this holy presence is assembled to help us do the work God has called us to do. Step out then in confidence and do not be afraid to try something new. The host of heaven stands beside you, the creative Spirit watches. Be bold in acts of love, be brave in daring to hope: rise up on the light that surrounds you.

June 6

Hope does not fall from the sky. It is a feeling made as often as found. We generate hope. We create it and share it and sustain it with our own determination. With every breath we take in life we have another moment to express our hope in what is to come. Our hope is not a wish, but a commitment. To say we have given up hope means that we have given up our willingness to keep producing it. God keep us from such resignation. God give us the spirit to always be a source of hope, a life of hope, for all to see and share.

June 7

I see the beauty in you, even though you laugh when I say it. I see it there in your eyes, that innocent gaze that still looks for what is good, that searches a glimpse of heaven in streets where strangers pass unspeaking. I see the beauty of your soul still linger over a human need long left to save itself. I see it in the movement of your hands reaching out to grasp what others will not touch. You have not lost the beauty within, even after all these years in the fields of our shared struggle. It is who you are. It is what you mean to me.

June 8

Itouched the light of heaven, just the other day, standing in a hospital room, praying protection for a man about to step into an unknown. It was the strangest feeling. As the prayer was spoken the words turned to streams of light, weaving like a ribbon around the patient, until he was radiant in the glow of God's love. That light-filled prayer remains even now, in these quiet morning shadows. I speak those words with you in mind, a prayer for your safekeeping. Don't be surprised if when you catch a glimpse in a mirror you imagine you see a halo.

June 9

What compensation can you offer for the loss of a dream? There is none. We negotiate our aging as best we can, bargaining our way through illness and loss, celebrating the joys we have received, mourning the passing of our friends, watching the edge of time move closer. It is not youth that we grieve, but rather the what might have been. How often the mind wanders to where it longed to be. May God protect your dream. May God help you find it. May what you hope to see still be seen, and what you hoped to do be the final bow at the close of your play.

June 10

Have you ever looked out at the star-filled night and thought how very small we are? I think we all have. Or stood by the shore or beneath mountains or beside a great canyon: we are only a tiny flicker of life adrift in a reality beyond the scope of our dreaming. And yet, as small as we may be, look at what great works we can do. We can endure the worst hardships and never lose our faith. We can carry the deepest burdens and never complain. We can love with such power and passion that our love never ends. Small we may be, but no mountain could ever laugh half as hard as we.

June 11

God grant to every lonely heart a special measure of grace. May all those we have lost in life, all those who were precious parts of our story, be lifted up before us once again, embraced by the love of our memory. We all will taste the bitter water of grief, we will all know what it means to let someone go. But only for the blink of an eye. Only for an instant. Like dolphins dancing on the sea, we will rise as one to play beneath a different sun, far from sorrow's distant shore. So be blessed today all who remember, be comforted and reassured. You have loved and will love again.

June 1 2

Joy flows like honeyed light around the one who feels it, accepts it, believes it. Joy as grand as unconditional love or as simple as being loved in return. Joy in waking to a new day, joy in sleeping beneath the peace of angels. Joy is the work of God completed, the goal of God's coming, the purpose of God's partnership with any human heart open enough to search for wonder. May you know this joy in your life. May you embrace the gift of hope it brings and know that it was meant for you. May joy encircle you in the light of love and hold you safe from the shadows of sorrow.

June 1 3

Leadership without humility is like love without compassion. We are each called to exercise the authority entrusted to us by God. We are asked to share our vision, our experience, our wisdom. When we do so, we are leaders who empower others to lead in their own way. We are a key in the hand of God used for that moment to unlock the gifts of those who are our peers in mission. True spiritual leadership then is not exercised from on high, but from within the center of community. There are no thrones in the house of God, but many chairs around a common table.

June 14

The meditations of my heart are the words I write each morning. Guided by unseen currents, the stillness and the prayer, scribbling quietly before the dawn, to find the meaning waiting at the far edge of every night. I do not know how well these words will serve the purpose to which they are printed, but truth is never tame and justice never content. So I write what my heart reveals: blessed are you who believe without judgment, who love without condition, who act without reward, who give without prompting, who pray without ceasing, who dance without the need of music.

June 15

Keep your balance. In all you do, in all you decide, in all you dream, keep your spiritual balance. How often life comes to that: walking the wire over a sea of troubles. We step out in hope and fear, not sure how to make it to the other side. In times like this let your internal gyroscope of faith, your trust in the One who holds you steady, guide your every step. Do not be anxious. Do not look down. But fix your eyes on where you most need to be. Walk by faith and let the hands of holy angels hold you up until you touch the solid ground of a love forever enduring.

J u n e   1 7

I had a woman once tell me that she cringed to call God her Father, not because of gender, but because her own father had been far from perfect. The image brought home a painful memory. May God redeem the place of fathers in all our lives. If the memory is happy, let that a gentle blessing be. But if the thought stirs shades of emotion, then let this healing truth bring peace: what is missing from our lives will one day be restored. That empty space will be filled by a love as pure as any parent can provide, a love that frees the heart of a child to sing.

J u n e   1 8

A short list from the disciple's handbook. To have an alternative in mind before we question the plan on the table. To value brevity and clarity as much as getting to speak. To practice common sense as the measure of what we call vision. To be as gracious in dealing with the mistakes of others as we are in acknowledging our own. To practice justice in small ways close to home as much as proclaiming it for others far away. To stay for the cleanup crew every time we sit at the head table. To know that frequent applause is a sign that it is time to share the spotlight.

June 19

Sanctuary. The house of God that shelters all those who come in need. Let our communities of faith be sanctuary for any who seek safe space simply to be who they are. Let our walls be a refuge against intolerance and fear, our welcome a healing hand to restore the dignity of every human heart. Let our doors be ever open, O God, to protect your children from harm. Give us the courage to be the sanctuary for others that you have been for us, the one place we knew we could go when the dark clouds gathered and the hearth of our hope grew cold. Sanctuary.

June 20

If you are tired from all your labors, burned out by doing what you think you have to do: I pray for you. If you are unsure which way to turn, lost in a maze of choices that offer no clear path forward: I pray for you. If you are carrying the weight of a need, a burden of love for others whose lives are at odds and whose dreams are on hold: I pray for you. Rest for the weary, vision for the seeker, strength for the care-giver, all this I pray and more. For you, I pray, with all my heart I pray, and will always pray, until my day is done.

June 21

I will not mince words when I name two of the great forces against which we must contend. Greed and fear. They have stalked the dark forests of our souls for longer than we have memory. They are primal, persistent, powerful, ever seeking to subvert the will of God. They exist in every human culture and from them none of us is immune. But if we name them, if we turn the clear light of truth on them, they shrink in size and wither before the justice of heaven. We need to turn that light on now. We need to be light-keepers through the storm to come.

June 22

As someone who has spent many long years on the road, I know the value, the joy, of simply coming home. Home is the belonging we create for one another out of the empty air of an indifferent world. It is warmth spun into space, the familiar sounds and smells of our own small tribe, the feel of acceptance draped over our shoulders, the calm confusion of life being lived and lived as we like it. Home. It comes in all shapes and sizes. It fits the family that makes it. May God bless your home. May God bless where you dwell and all those for whom you long when you are away.

J u n e   2 4

One of the nice things about being a bishop who visits parishes is that I can say things that the local leaders find a little more difficult. For example: yes, stewardship is about more than money, but, it is also still about money. These days, like most days, our corner parishes are in need of financial support. I pray that we all give as generously as we can. Pledge to the place where you worship and discover the wonderful feeling of giving until it feels good. The love of money may be the root of all evil, but the need for money is the root of all that pays the bills.

J u n e   2 5

Late in the midnight of my dreams I saw the great throng of those who long for a healing touch gathered on a field of endless need. Silent they stood and waited with eyes more eloquent in patient prayer than all the words of comfort could fulfill. I am alone I thought and in the first phases of despair realized how little I could do. Then on the rush of mighty wings the Great Spirit came and caught me up and lifted me high to see. Beneath Her wings healing grace spread like starlight and fell like first snow until not one was left untouched. Not one. Not even one.

June 26

God, let me hear what is being said to me today. Let me not miss something important to another person because I am too distracted by myself. Help me to listen. Not with impatience or pre-conceived attitudes or my own quick response already in my verbal holster, but listen with an open mind and a desire to learn, with compassion and with humility. Free me from speech as though it were only a tool and not a doorway. Let my listening be my love turned outward, my soul reaching out to embrace, my heart taking in the truth with the joy of discovery.

June 27

I sometimes think the only thing of value I have ever been able to make are the memories I have created. They say that when we pass from this life to the next it is the memories we have that are all we truly take with us. As I grow older I believe it is true for I find myself watching many of the things I thought important diminish and change, while my memories of people and places become all the more precious. I wince at the ones that still bring me pain, but smile to the core of my soul at the ones that embody love. Memory is what I have and who I will one day be.

June 28

In a few days I will go to a great church convention to sign my little book of hope. I will be one person among ten thousand. I will be there only for a day. And yet I pray my book is a blessing beyond all of the budgets and debates and resolutions. I pray it as a single seed of renewal. Renewal comes not through human effort but by the grace of God. When we trust in the Spirit and walk humbly before our Creator, when we love without rules and give without reward, we are transformed. In simple words of hope like these a single truth can set ten thousand souls to sing.

June 29

Sometimes all we need is strength to make it through another day. Sometimes we are not sure we have that strength. When your burdens become too great and you have given so much there is not much left to give, then take this prayer and put it in your pocket for when you need it most. May the breath of life, the first breath, the gift of God to all that moves under heaven, come into you and renew your spirit. Be strong again, not with grim determination, but quiet confidence. Be refreshed in a healing love over which no darkness will ever prevail.

JULY

July 1

Your faith has made you well. Against all odds, against all assaults on your health or happiness, against the kind of news you cannot accept but cannot escape. Your faith has seen you through. It has given you courage. It has allowed you to help those you love and offered you hope when hope was more precious than gold. Faith has kept you safe and lifted you up and made you laugh and shown you the wonder that is your life, the joy that is your inheritance. Go in peace today and never be afraid. Your faith has made you well.

July 2

We thank you, God, for our mentors, for those good and wise women and men who came into our lives to mold us with their kindness, wisdom and example. Thank you for our teachers, the truth-tellers, who helped us see what otherwise we would have missed. Thank you for the counselors and colleagues who kept us honest, shared our sorrows, gave us the help we needed when times were hard and tomorrow uncertain. There are so many you have sent to stand beside us. So many hands to shape the clay that first you fashioned and still you seek to form.

J u l y   3

I have seen the far shores of tomorrow. I have seen the shape of what will come move like Balinese puppets against the flickering screen of time. I have known the what and the why before the question ever was asked. But to see clearly within, into the nature of my own soul, to know why I am or why I choose to do what I do, that sight is ever clouded, a mystery beyond my reckoning. We all may have our vision, a grace of imagination God given, but few are seers of their own spirit or prophets of their own desire. Those rivers run too deep, their source the holy well of creation.

J u l y   4

Say it. Say it for no reason at all and when least expected. Say it before it is too late, before time passes you by and you wish you had said it when you had the chance. Say it to her now. Say it to him. To the kids, to the grandkids, to nieces and nephews, to grandparents, to all sorts and conditions of relations, even and perhaps most especially if those lines of relation are stretched a little thin. Say it to dear friends, to those who have been with you longer than you can remember, to those who tell you with their eyes they want to hear it. Say it: I love you.

July 5

Believe today in all the good you have done, in all the good you have been, in all the good you are each and every day you wake to do what God has called you to do. Believe in your vocation and your vision. Let the simple goodness within you transcend all doubt and transform all frailty. You are not called to be perfect, but to be true in heart and deed. Believe in yourself. You have touched the lives of many and left your mark of hope for all the world to see. Believe in the good you are and be the good you believe.

July 6

I have a time machine. I would be glad to take you for a ride if you need a change. It is easy to use and very safe. I can even promise to have you home by supper. Just meet me by the garden gate. We will walk out to the sparkling stream that runs beneath the shade of ancient trees. If we take the path under their sheltering arms we will come to a quiet pool where we can kick off our shoes and dangle our feet in cool water. With the blue sky above and only the clouds to listen we can slip away from our electronic today to rest in the peace of a more gentle past.

July 8

Living in community is an earned blessing. It does not just happen. Communities are formed when people recognize that they share a common vision and move toward one another to see that vision more clearly. Community is maintained when people have the integrity to be honest, patient, accountable and forgiving with one another. Spiritual community does not require that every member believes the same thing. It does require that what they believe allows them to respect and work with those who believe differently. Community is love made visible by intention.

July 9

Trust your instincts on this one, be guided by your spiritual intuition. There are times when either there is not enough evidence to go on, or, there are so many facts that the walls of reason cannot contain them. When you face this kind of uncertainty, let your inner light be your guide. It has grown over years of experience. It has been developed by your own deep reflection, the wisdom of a street smart spiritual sense. Take a deep breath. Offer your hand to God in prayer and step out with faith to do what you feel is right.

J u l y   1 0

We are only small lights, you and I, making our way through what often seems a world consumed in darkness. We are not able to shine the sunlight of God's radiant love, but generate all the brightness we can with the little measure of hope and love given for us to share. We are small lights, you and I, but far from insignificant, for when we gather with our friends, dancing in the darkness, we are the fireflies of a summer night, enchanting the evenings, tiny constellations, blinking out messages of joy, the innocent delight of our child-hearted creator.

J u l y   1 1

Was it all worth it? I think age has something to do with how we answer. When I was younger I might have been tempted to say no. The losses and griefs of life seemed sharper then, the younger skin of my soul more tender to the unexpected hurt of a reality I still imagined I could control. But the years have seasoned my experience, shown me the fine point lessons between the lines of loss, helped me to see a longer view than the moment before me. Was it all worth it? Yes, says my elder heart, yes because I would not be what I have become without it.

July 12

G od help me not to walk backwards through life. Keep me from being so focused on what is past that I fail to savor what is present or imagine what is to come. Let me learn my lessons that I may not repeat my own history of mistakes. Let me reflect on past glories but with enough humility to know they are memories not mandates. Free me from lingering regret, anger too long carried, hurt that haunts my dreams and steals the joy from what I should now cherish as your healing gift. Turn my face forward, God, that I may better see you coming to meet me.

July 13

F ew things make us feel more helpless than the onset of sudden illness or medical need. It comes like a whirlwind, rising up, dark and menacing, scattering all before it, leaving you fragile and afraid. I have stood with others in the face of many such storms, holding the ground of hope, praying the fear to peace, driving back the evil winds of sickness and sorrow. And so once again, on the rock of all that I believe, I stretch out my faith against the gale, with any and all who need this prayer, and I cry comfort, healing and peace, until the wind subsides and the sky clears.

July 15

In these quiet hours I pray a rosary of special intention for all those I know who are in need of blessing. Some beads are by name, a single person I see so clearly, even if only for a moment. Some are for names I do not know, the hungry, the homeless, the ones in harm's way. Some are communities. Some are calls for justice, some are whispers of mercy. But all of these beads are living souls, bound together by the thread of God's love, linked by that love, held fast by the chain of prayer. In these quiet hours my rosary circles the Earth while never leaving my hand.

July 16

If I were a gambling man I would be willing to bet that you know someone in your spiritual circle who suffers from depression. Could even be you. Could even be me. I am no gambler and certainly no doctor, so I will not lightly name this condition for another. All I know is that faith communities are shelters for so many who know the meaning of shadows in sunlight. The church is our sanctuary. Let us open this irony to healing truth: the house of thanksgiving is home to many who sorrow. When we see one another clearly, we have the chance to share a smile.

July 17

Our Teacher was asked, what is truth? I have tried all my life to answer. It is what I know in my heart, but cannot grasp with my mind. It is where I take my stand, but often find myself at sea. It is what I see so clearly that looks so different to others. It is what I try to tell, unless it is better to withhold. It is what sets me free, but constrains me. It is unchanging, but ever growing. It is as great as the Spirit, and as small as a childhood lesson. It is what we spend a lifetime seeking to discern, and recognize in an instant. Truth is the nature of God, the infinite within.

July 18

Have no fear, not of all the small things that crowd in around you, hemming you in like insistent weeds, making you feel overwhelmed by the details of life, the endless rounds you make as the watchman of your own world. Have no fear, not of the great things that come upon you unexpected, the life changers, the avalanche of need in your reality or that of those you love. No thing, great or small, no change, no detail, no power can hold you captive or control your life. Look up. Behold the light coming to you, clearing every shadow before it, and have no fear.

July 19

Anger is a weight that keeps the soul from flying. It grounds us to walk the all too familiar paths of passion. We lose the ability to listen but wait impatiently to spring our next words like a trap. We feel the fire in the belly of blame and see through its heat only a distorted image of the truth we used to share. Anger seeks to control, to dominate, to demand. God save us from its dead power. God free us from its heavy hand. Let our souls regain their flight, light in spirit, open in mind, gentle in word and deed, that we may see and love more clearly in the clean air of your mercy.

July 20

How kind it was for you to remember me. After all these years, through all these changes, in spite of all these shifts in both our lives that have carried us so far apart. Still you keep the line of love between us firmly in your hand, gently in your heart. The bond of friendship is a sacrament uncounted but still ever sacred. It is entrusted to us by God to share our faithfulness in time as well as thought. Your act of gracious spirit is the outward and visible sign of the goodness that shines so brightly within. How kind, old friend, it was, and is, and ever shall be.

July 22

Take the long road. Like you, there have been times in my life when I have been tempted to look for a short cut to where I wanted to go. Our human nature seeks the easy way out, the instant gratification, the fast lane to our destination. To make matters worse, we live in a culture that encourages us to try it and rewards us if we get away with it. But pardon an old man's old school advice: there is only one path to take and that is the path of integrity. If you cut corners you may arrive sooner, but you will have lost yourself along the way.

July 23

Let the logic of love make sense of senseless loss, that those who weep in wonder of a pain which defies understanding will not be left to mourn alone, but feel the comfort of a people at prayer, the truth that life is greater than any sorrow will ever subdue. And let those prayers be the dawn of their namesake city, reaching out to touch every grieving heart, reaching out to bring light and peace and hope to every innocent family weighted by violence, that they will find the strength to believe again in a mercy that soothes dark memories with a love never ending.

July 24

Faith grows in organic patterns. It is process. Be mindful of these patterns and you will delight in watching the energy of faith moving you forward in the knowledge of God. For example: listen and you will learn, learn and you will know, know and you will see, see and you will believe, believe and you will trust, trust and you will love, love and you will give, give and you will receive, receive and you will have, have and you will hold, hold and you will keep, keep and you will become, become and you will be what God intended when you first listened to the Word.

July 25

All my relatives. Every living creature. Every bird that flies, every fish that swims, every animal that walks the Earth: they are all my relatives. In the great family of God the spirals of kinship weave us all into relationship, mutual, caring, connected. Since all that God does is done in love, so all that God created was created in love. There are no orphans left standing alone, for all are embraced by the common compassion of a common Creator. How well we treat our siblings is how well we honor our Maker. Every heart that beats, beats praises to our God.

July 26

Tired. Just feeling tired. How often that single little word writes a book about how we feel. Eyes that burn, shoulders that ache, every step made in Frankenstein shoes. Run down, burned up. Over worked, under slept. And all the while circumstances conspire to keep us there, never enough time to get the rest we need. For all who are sleep walkers on the job of life I offer this blessing: be absolved of all reason not to stop, be free of every burden, curl up into healing covers of peace, let renewal of body and spirit lift you up with energy restored, tired no more.

July 27

I drove through Comanche country, yellow grass and endless sky, to see my mentor, my Choctaw mother, mind younger than tomorrow, soul older than the wind. I drove with my Caddo elder, a second sacred woman, spirit quick like lightning. We sat in a circle through timeless hours, speaking softly of what matters. And what great thoughts did we share, what theology did we discuss? A small dog held in a grandmother's lap, a tiny heart beating its drum against illness: we loved that little life, we loved what we had, that our love could reach the endless sky.

J u l y   2 9

L ast night beneath the moon, within the circle of many tribes, the drum sounding like a heartbeat, my family by my side, I knew what it meant to belong. This was my story. These were my companions on a path walked by many ancestors of the same spirit. I pray that all who read these words will be blessed by belonging. May you belong, to your own story, people, and place. May you feel your part in a community by birth or adoption. May you know your ancestors and may they know you. May you be embraced by family, ever in the circle of those who know you best.

J u l y   3 0

I t is time for me to prepare my sacrifice to God. How strange those old words sound today. Not only because they stir the vague memory of sheep and oxen brought to the temple, but even more because they reverse the expectation that I am on the receiving end of sacrifice. In this age, we do not like to give up anything. We like to get. But a spiritual life requires a spirit of sacrifice, the deep sense of sharing, of humility, of balance that denies the feel good promise of constant reward and calls us to account for what we return to life that life may give to all.

July 31

A quiet spirit rests within you, though you live in a world of words. You are practiced in the art of our time, navigating the white water of words that carries us racing through days as if we needed to out run the sun, balancing information as you sort the worthless from the real, plugged in to communicate with electronic gizmos that grow old before you buy them. The noise alone deafens language to monkey chatter, a civilization seduced by its own need to talk, and talk, and talk. But deep within, deep in your soul, the silent spirit still lingers beside a pool of dark water untroubled.

AUGUST

August 1

The dreams of youth never die. They are immortal. Even if we did not become what we once imagined, those visions of innocent inspiration remain as suns in the small galaxies of hope that spin forever in our internal universe. They give birth to other realities, the planets of what we do now, the hard core ground of our being. So do not despair if you did not dance the prima part, pitch at Fenway, write the great global novel, or become the next Thomas Merton. Those dreams birthed the best of you and live on in all you do.

August 2

Grandmother God rose last night in the face of the full moon. I stood out in the still summer heat watching her. How pale you look I said. How hot you look she said. We shared a smile. Knowing God is seeing God where you find her. In images and languages and the thousand faces of her world. In the intuition of faith we find her more clearly than in the narrow lines of our theology. Her scandal is an intimacy with all of us who are her family, who call her by many names, and stand outside on hot summer nights to greet her when she comes to call.

August 3

The bitter taste of disappointment lingers long after the moment has past, a faded memory but one that haunts the hidden hallways of the heart, appearing from the shadows when least expected, to remind us of the sad imperfection of the spiritual community we call home. How many have been hurt by the church? How many have left? How many have stayed but carry the scar? To all who know this story, I offer a hand of healing. You are not alone, but one among many. Come help us build a home where this hurt does not happen.

August 5

When I was a child, the old-timers used to say there was nothing you could do about the weather. When my grandchild is my age, the old-timers will say there was something we could do about the weather, but didn't. Weather is not a force of magic beyond our control, but a system into which we can make our entry. Climate change, global warming, is real. Our challenge is not melting ice or burning crops, but the greed that keeps us standing still while our world falls down around us. God help us to act before it is too late, God forgive us if we choose not to try.

August 6

Here in the dark, when dawn is only a promise, I pray a thread of light. I hold it in my hands, asking God to infuse it with all that is bright and hopeful. With healing and grace, with mercy and love, with truth and justice. A shining cord of prayer, a life-line of prayer, a flowing light that weaves through the darkness from one heart to another. I send out this prayer to make its way to any in need. Take hold as it passes by, feel the warm within, and know that you are connected not only to those who pray your name but to the One who called you by name before you ever were born.

August 7

The elders used to say that God is very thrifty because God does not like to throw anything away. Instead, God prefers to mend things. At the age I am now I know this to be true. I have had a broken heart, broken dreams, broken trust, broken spirit and a broken body. But each and every time, God has mended me. With patience and persistence, with a careful hand and a keen eye, God has put me back together, knit the pieces with the bond of love, restored them through grace, that I might once again be useful and help in my own fashion the healing of others.

A u g u s t   8

S illy little Death, stop your fussing now, hush and don't make such a scene, we all know you well enough, so don't think you can scare anyone by pouting or playing grim. Yes, you are part of this family, and yes, we all respect you, but you must not think too highly of yourself or imagine you are the boss of your siblings, of Life or Love, of Joy and Light, or any of the playful children whose games you want to spoil. Go to your room now, read a good book, and have yourself a time out. If you behave, when the call comes, I will let you walk me home.

A u g u s t   9

B e mindful of how impatience has become a mark of our culture. We are impatient with our elders, bored with their stories, as if they were not our own. Impatient with our children, anxious that they achieve before they can walk. Impatient with others, demanding ever faster means of receiving shorter answers. Impatient with ourselves, never enough hours in the day to do all we imagine we must accomplish to keep up with the world around us. Impatience is the symptom. Regard it well. It shows us who we are, if we will take time enough to see.

August 10

There is a word within you that needs to be spoken. It may be a word of comfort or forgiveness, of affirmation or love, of truth or insight. It may be something you should have said long ago, or something that has just come to you. Whatever it is, it is waiting to be released. It has the power to help and heal, to open doors for another person, perhaps for a whole community. Pray for God's guidance in showing you just how to say it. Take a deep breath of the Spirit. And then open your heart and set your captive wisdom free to change life for the better.

August 12

I walk by faith, but I do not walk with my eyes closed. Faith does not mean I am blind to the world around me. In fact, just the reverse. Faith makes me even more aware of reality. It opens my eyes to hunger, poverty, injustice and prejudice. It offers me a vision of the beauty of creation and demands that I be held accountable for preserving that vision. I see God alive and active all around me. I am a witness to the living truth of a love so clear I cannot look away. Walk by faith and you walk with eyes wide open both to what is without and to what is within.

August 13

I hope you know the story of the nuns who would not be silent or bow their heads to the demands of men who sought to control them. It is important to us all for it reminds us that the church is not a palace where some must enter by the back door to serve the few who matter, but rather we are a community of free human beings who stand together as equals before the God who made us all. The witness of our sisters to the dignity of every person is a bell sounding change and hope to all who will listen. These women point the way, let us rejoice and join them.

August 14

Be blessed today, blessed in who you are, in the time you are, in the place you are. Blessed in your moment of rising, when what waits for you still waits, either good or bad, so that you may face it knowing you are not alone. Blessed in your acts of creation, great and small, the things you will do to make a world for yourself, doing all that you can to make that world a better place. Blessed in your hours of resting, when you seek to leave it all behind, embracing the peace of angels who watch over you, keeping you blessed while the quiet stars shine above you.

August 15

Thank God I am not God for if I were God then God would no God be. That odd little phrase ran through my prayers like a church mouse at play. It danced its way past deeper thoughts, tapping out a rhythm of reason to make a mantra so simple it must be true. I share it for any who, like me, may want a gentle reminder that titles and privilege, education and position, income and housing, race and gender, age and status have no spiritual qualities inherent within them. I am not holy or wise by birthright but by the grace of the One who bears the Name.

August 16

It happened again. As I recited the names of those who need healing in procession of my prayer, I saw the candles flicker, the breeze move unseen in a room enclosed, the presence of hope rise up like the Spirit summoned. I turn my prayers outward. I join my heart to yours. For every person I know, for the millions I will never know, I offer the power of a pure intention, the mercy of unconditional love, the healing grace of those who sit and wait with deep expectation. Be healed. Be whole. Be safe in an embrace that will never let you go. Let it happen again.

August 17

S tand tall today. Breathe in the strength of the Spirit, be renewed in heart and mind, consider well the lessons life has taught you, feel the truth of justice whispering in your ear, and reach out with your hands to take hold of the work God has entrusted to you, let your voice ring out bright and clear, proclaim the acceptable moment of a holy hope, be the example others are praying to see, not timid, but confident, full of faith, full of compassion, alive in love without judgment or shame, giving all you can with all you have to all you meet. Stand tall today.

August 19

W here we stand is never solid. What we call reality changes shape without our bidding or our control. There are times when we wake to find the world a vast expanse, open and full of wonder, ours for the fun of it all. Then again the whole of the universe contracts into a single room, a single night, a single moment of longing prayer. The space within which we live is fluid and ever shifting. One thing only is sure, the rock on which we stand, the very ground of our being: God of unchanging love, God of compassion constant, God of endless mercy, God of our every hour.

August 20

Come dance with me, out in the backyard, under the stars, where the fireflies pretend they are Japanese lanterns, and the dogs keep time to the music with their tails, and the neighbors peep from upstairs windows to wonder again if we have taken leave of our senses, because yes, yes we have, we have left the knotted frowns of sorrow to sit dumbly before the incessant TV of our time, and gone to waltz back the magic of love that always waits for those who dare to seek it, out in the backyard, under the stars, beneath the kindly old moon who married us.

August 21

It is not the promise that I could live forever that won my heart to God, for to be honest there are times I am not sure I would want that gift even though it is offered. It is not the promise I will be forgiven, for as gracious as that may be, in my heart I doubt there are some things it could cover. No, what took my breath away was something a little less grand, but a promise I have found I have treasured most. When you need me, God said, I will be there. No matter what. No matter when. I will be there. A promise both given and kept: to a soul like mine, it is enough.

August 22

Not all peace passes our understanding. For example there is the peace between nations. The peace between religions. These are needs for peace we can understand and support. There is the need to stop violence against women, against LGBT people, against anyone based on race or creed. That's very clear. Peace for refugees, for the oppressed, for the poor of every land. We can understand all of that. Peace in the home. Peace in family. Peace in mind and heart. We understand peace because we are peacemakers. That's our job. That's our faith. That's our witness.

August 23

I work the graveyard shift of prayer, the nights that seem empty to some, but to those with a burdened heart, the nights that never end. I stay alert to the midnight call of the soul, the cry of one far away, whose spirit voice reaches out through deserted streets, to find someone, anyone, who can help remove the pain. I do not keep my vigil because I am good, but because, like you, I have been there, to the all night cafe, where you go when you just don't want to be alone. Can you stay awake with me, God asked, and yes, we said, yes, we can, this time, we can.

August 24

Come outside, I have something I want to show you. Come out from being bent by work, hunched over a screen, reading checkbooks like hieroglyphics, cleaning what you just cleaned, carrying the load for others, tending to the needs that never end, managing the details, waiting in line, sighing for lost chances, quarreling with fate your imaginary friend, listening for the phone, making a meal for one, hurrying in ever smaller circles. Stop all of that and come outside. I have a world to show you, a life to show you, that has been waiting for you, waiting too long. Come outside.

August 26

I come before you, God, to stand with all of my sisters and brothers who face the basic need to make a living. I ask you to look upon us with your favor. I pray for those looking for work. I pray for those working but still in financial need. For moonlighters and paycheck stretchers, for the working poor. For those one illness away from poverty. For the ones with educational debt. For those on fixed incomes. For the good people laid off, for families strained by money worry, for those at the end of their hope. Help your people, O God, give them honest work for honest pay.

August 27

You were born to bless. It is in your nature. It is a deep part of your calling. Do not shy from this gift because you believe it is reserved only for the few. Blessing is a birthright of all who believe. Open your spirit to those around you, to those near, to those far away. Let your heart hold them in the inner light and your mind be still as a pool of wind free water. Pray quietly the words of your blessing, send it out from an outstretched hand to wrap around them and keep them safe. Use the love entrusted to you to change the lives of all who shelter beneath your care.

August 28

How must I look to you, O God, coming to you every Sunday, dressed in all my pomp and circumstance? Beneath my robes do you not see me, a little boy with a scraped knee, so proud he survived the loss of a tooth, with dirty fingernails and grass stains on his knees? As a child I began this journey. As a child I shall reach journey's end. No need for vanity along the way. No need for pretense or ego or any of the brave fronts we put on to impress ourselves before time's patient mirror. Beneath it all the One who made us sees us for who we are and always shall be.

August 29

Just when I think it is over, just when I am sure there is nothing before me but the still dark seas of resignation, along you come, a fresh wind from an unexpected direction, billowing out the sails of hope, waking me up from sorrow's slumber, and setting me in motion once again to guide my own fate toward some distant shore where I can see lights on my horizon and the sounds of bells ringing me homeward bound. For those moments, I am eternally grateful, O God, for only you command the wind, only you breathe life over the deepest water.

August 30

Ok, pop quiz: name one of your favorite teachers. If coming up with an answer was easy, then join me in pausing for a moment to reflect on the gift that those who teach are in our lives. We still remember our best teachers because they were such a blessing, not just for the knowledge they gave us, but for the way they gave it. They inspired us. They gave us confidence and pride and a sense of adventure. They changed us. It is a national crime that we do not value our teachers more than we do. They give so much and receive so little. God bless them all

August 31

Great trees bow their heads when the God of Hosts passes by, the proud mountains tremble and the clouds gather to pour out their life giving rain upon the dry earth. When the Creator of All walks the land the rivers run swift to sparkling seas and flocks of birds sweep in dance beneath the sun. The majesty of our Sovereign hushes the wind and bids the night to cover her face before she spreads a shawl of stars around her feet. But our God is never more mighty, more wonderful, than when God stops to hold a child in need, whispering hope into a longing heart.

SEPTEMBER

September 2

You were born with the gift of empathy, though at times you have wondered if it is a gift or a burden. As a child you felt the swirl of emotions around you as if they were as common as color. In adolescence the intensity often left you speechless. But now you strive to let what others imprint on you be a source of healing, an art not a science of compassion. One mark of the spiritual life is the ability to share deeply in the feelings of others, without the hubris of imagining you have lived their story, but with the honesty to engage both joy and pain as our human handprint.

September 3

Down the darker hallways of my heart, where I very rarely go, there are rooms long closed off, the still rooms of memories past, places where sorrow lingers, a sudden draft beneath the door, that chills me to my core, and steals my smiles away. I know you have rooms like these. We all do. So I take this moment to brave the shadows, to speak openly of what remains behind closed doors, to stretch out my hand of prayer, the honest hand of hope, the steady hand of love, to guide you back from dim passages of your past, and lighten your home with laughter.

September 4

I rise to sing the joy of simply being human. I do not deny the pain I have known, the losses and the grief, but I will not let bitterness be all that I taste of life. There are too many sunsets that leave me standing still before their beauty, too many babies wheeled by in strollers that make me smile, too much love in the eyes I see from faces wrinkled by time but timeless in their wisdom. All of creation calls me to celebrate. All of life invites me to dance. Therefore I choose to carry my pain with head held high and walk the blessing way until the last lights fade.

September 5

Show us the way, O God, show us the path to follow. So often it comes down to this, knowing which way to go. And it is so easy for us to be uncertain, we have journeyed for so long to get so far that we have forgotten just how we did it. The layers of choice are deep in the old soil of memory. The options blow the leaves all around the yard. Give us vision to see more clearly what is before us. Give us wisdom to take the right steps. Give us courage to follow where truth will lead. And let the journey bring us ever closer to you, our destination the cause of our beginning.

September 6

I am hunger. I am hunger, walking city streets, passing by all the well dressed, well fed, well-heeled shoppers with money enough to spend and time enough to kill. I am hunger, unseen in the small places, the backwater places, the hidden places of a polished nation whose polished politicians talk a good game but only make more of me. I am hunger, in a world that huddles up, hides out, walks for days, dodges gunfire, lives in drought, has the U.N. for a mother and a refugee tag for a burial. I am hunger, sitting under a bridge, with no one to talk to, but Jesus.

September 7

Do you see what I see, when you look out over the landscape of your life? Do you see the many faces of love, the faces of friends and family who have stood by you through struggles long past and who will stand with you still come what may? Do you see the faithful angels, patient and caring, watching your horizon against all alarms? Do you see your ancestors, gathered in the half-light of long ago but shining ever through the night, blessing you and blessing you again? Do you see the hearth of God, a beacon from home, a promise unbroken? Do you see what I see?

September 9

Untangle my mind, O God, with patience gently pull out all the threads that have knotted themselves into a ball and left me tired of thinking. Surely reason is among your greatest gifts, but with its use comes a peril. Like so many I can over-think my problems, worrying them into fine bits or blowing them up out of proportion. I let my monkey mind chase me around in circles. Calm my thoughts, I pray. Still my spinning imagination and bring me back to that quiet pool at the center of my soul. Let me in peace ponder what I need to know and with a clear mind find my question's answer.

September 10

Be renewed in your faith as you read these words. Be brought back to that moment when you first believed, that fresh, new, hopeful moment when you realized that God was real. Let tired resignation and numbing routine fall from your shoulders like leaves in autumn drifting away on the clean wind of the Spirit. Be lifted up. Be confirmed. Be whole. Allow the healing love of gentle power to move through you. Draw deep the breath of life that has seemed so long in coming. Awake now to the promise within you. Be renewed in your faith. Let the mystery happen.

September 11

The Teacher said we cannot serve two masters, but these days it often seems we have more than two. The demands of work and home are never ending. The need to make ends meet, the pressure of school, promises made that must be kept, the cell phone ringing, things to fix, things to buy, driving in circles for the sake of others, answering that next text, even keeping an eye on this every hungry screen. How many masters do we serve? The core of the spiritual life is the uncluttered mind. Who we serve is not a list of needs, but the one still point of love that fulfills every need.

September 12

A messenger I have met before came to take me on midnight wings to a high place where you can see more clearly the far reaches of time. We stood unseen before a restless world, people moving like waves of troubled water, the commerce of earnest lives spent building a maze of meaning. She waved her hand. Only an oasis remained beneath the moon in the midst of endless dunes. This alone is real, she said, love shared and received. When all the business of your life is concluded what will remain? Love alone has the water of life, all else a mirage beneath the moon.

September 13

HELLO, My Name Is...I put on the ubiquitous church meeting name tag today because I am meeting myself. Again. In my Native American culture my ancestors changed their name to signal that they had become something new. There is wisdom there because in our lifetimes we grow, we evolve, we learn. We become someone new. Spiritual life is an unfolding. An awakening. It is self-revelation. We go deeper. We make discoveries about who we are and why we are. We become a new creation, perhaps more than once. Time to meet who you will be.

September 14

WHEN I began writing these thoughts in the hour of prayer before each dawn there were four others who were part of this circle with me. Soon there will be two thousand. And how many others join us when these words are shared in other places I cannot count. I pause to give thanks for this witness because it has only happened by word of mouth, by one person at a time discovering grace by invitation. I thank God for each of you. The gift here is not what I write. It is that invitation. It is the way that each of us becomes a blessing, a call to hope, one person at a time.

September 16

I am lost to language on this day, struck silent with a humbled heart, to stand before the proof of simple kindness, that so knits our natures together, so embraces us as grown children of the same loving parent, that we put aside selfish cravings, the pretense of place, and rather reach with all we have to offer love, if even only for the moment. Call it hospitality, call it small acts of a gentle spirit, but mark well the power of kindness. When we are kind one to another, we are the arms of God holding fast the best of who we are and why we ever were made.

September 17

If, as a people, we want the world to see us as a place of promise and peace, then let us live by the light of our own example. Let us be welcoming to diversity, free of all prejudice, just to every person, rich or poor. Let our leaders be temperate in their speech, not adding to the anger of partisan rant, but calling our common spirit to a higher vision. Let our care for children be our measure, our lack of greed our pride, our integrity our greatest national treasure. Let the world see us practice what we preach and be blessed to do the same in their own way and manner.

September 18

Rise up and walk today, even if the path before you is one you dread. Rise up and feel renewed in your mind and body, even if you are confined to bed. Rise up and feel the cool wind of the Spirit lifting you over struggle and sorrow. Rise up and see your land of promise just beyond the river. Rise up and claim the justice that is yours by sacred right. Rise up and sing the praises of the One who set you free. Rise up and in your rising bring a thousand more to their feet. Rise up and shout joy into the Earth, hope and peace, love and love again. Rise up and walk today.

September 19

It happened again last night, a dream of healing so real that it has followed me into this morning. Therefore, I release it. I let it go into the early morning air, praying it on its way to find whoever needs it, praying it to come to rest on the windowsill of their soul. Be healed in your mind. Be healed in your spirit. Then let that healing move through your body to renew you in every way. Let this prayer be for you, or for someone you love. Let it be as real to you as it was to me, a vision of hope arising from shadow into light, riding on wings of faith to find you.

September 20

The best moments did not always seem that way at the time. Easy is not synonymous with good. Looking back I can see how my struggles have been transformative. They have offered me many lessons, even if the learning of them is something I would rather not do again. They showed me reality. They forced me to stretch with all my spiritual strength. They revealed the names of those on whom I could count. They made me wiser. The true character of my faith has not been shaped by comfort, but by the long nights when only God could help me find the dawn.

September 21

Come quietly to the end of this week. Come quietly to a moment of rest. Lay aside your anxious cares, put down your shouldered burden. Stretch your arms and legs, feel their tightness release. I know you have had a busy week; I know there is more to come tomorrow. But before you rush past me, hear my invitation. Come rest a moment. Come sit quietly by my side. Enter this small space of peace, this meditation embodied. All the busy world will wait, wait while we sit together, silent beneath a breeze that whispers: you were not made a machine but born to be a dreamer.

September 23

Please join me in this prayer of protection. Call it to mind from time to time so its energy may spread far and wide, a shield of light sustained by many souls. We pray protection for all in need of shelter. For innocent children that they may be safe from abuse, for youth in any danger, for women battered that they find freedom, for elders alone, for refugees, for first responders in the path of peril, for all soldiers far from home, for those who travel, for the ones with broken hearts, for any who need a place of peace beneath the wings of God: we pray the power of a holy protection.

September 24

Have you ever been surprised by a change in the weather? One morning you open the door and the feel of the air is different. One afternoon you step outside to see the clouds have arrived like unexpected guests at your door. We inhabit our small spaces of time as though they were permanent, lulled in our minds by the thought that what we have is all we get. We forget the seasons of God's grace, the changes that come upon us, the renewal, the freshening breeze, the longed for rain, the healing and the hope. Look up. Grace is the season you soon will see.

September 25

If I told you that an angel was standing beside you, would you believe me or would you laugh? If I said that there were streamers of light rising from places of prayer would you say yes or no? Would you call me mad if I confess that we do not always see with our eyes, but also with our faith? To see beauty where others see the outcast, to see hope and not despair, to see the Spirit moving on wings widespread, to see the dawn of peace even on the horizon of war: all of this and more is there to those whose vision is not doubt-clouded but by love made crystal clear.

September 26

What an uneasy generation we are, looking back to distant glory to add polish to faded dreams. Unsure of our leaders, unsure of our institutions, anxious that we may be losing a game we do not understand. We came, we saw, we consumed. That is no epitaph for a people who once felt freedom stir them to dare even ancient fears, to bend history to the shape of justice. Cry silence to politics that panders and open the hearts of the common citizen, that this great land will rise once more to be what at its best it might be, if truth were seen a virtue, peace a gift for all.

September 27

Give me the simple joys and I will be content. The peaceful evenings with those I love, watching the sun slip away to its rest. The laughter around the table, when all our cares seem to have lost their way and failed to appear. The long talks with old friends who know what I am saying before I say it. The magic of children's play, delighting only in delight. The devotion passed between me and a beloved pet when we cross that line of difference, bonded for life. The quiet hour of prayer when I not only know God is listening, but sitting right beside me.

September 28

May God's mercy come to you as a warm embrace on a cold day. May it wrap you up. Hold you close. May that divine embrace draw you so near that you can feel the heartbeat of time, the source of life, imprint itself into your soul. I pray this for you because I know what it feels like to stand naked in the cold. I have lived that sensory deprivation of loneliness, longing to be touched in any way that would not cause more pain. Be held in the everlasting arms. Be safe in a love that needs no words. May God's mercy come to you and abide with you and never let you go.

September 30

Want to help? Here's how: help your elders with listening, help your children with time, help your spouse with patience, help your friends with understanding, help your church with a pledge, help your co-workers with cheerfulness, help your community with volunteering, help the hungry with food, help the homeless with shelter, help the Earth with commitment, help the guilty with forgiveness, help the hurting with prayer, help the Spirit with energy, help the enclosed with a visit, help the addict with courage, help the bereaved with comfort, help yourself with the help of God.

OCTOBER

October 1

Loneliness follows age like a shadow. As the sun of life sets that shadow can grow ever longer. Old friends pass on, children move away, the house is sold, the familiar becomes the strange. Younger hearts may have trouble seeing it coming, for their sun sits high in a cloudless sky, but join me please in a compassionate prayer, all you who know the meaning of what I say. Loneliness can follow age to a still space, a place of naps and dreams, a solitary room, a sigh too deep for words. God let me cherish my elders, that their shadow be no longer than mine, in the light of your love.

October 2

Rise up, my soul, to sing. Rise up past all that would hold me down. Past age and illness, past loss and pain, past worry and fear. Rise up into a brighter light, a cleaner air, a place where I can see forever. Let the Earth roll in beauty before me, its mountains lavender and white before the sun, its rivers sparkling threads of ribbon blue. Let me rise up to behold a morning when peace will come at last and every heavy heart will be healed and every hungry life well fed. Lift me as light as falling snow caught on the wind of the Spirit. Rise up, my soul, and see how good life can be.

October 3

Open is a word that goes well with faith. Please God let us be open minded to the new lessons you may teach us every day about the mysteries of your meaning. Open hearted in compassion to one another without the pinched souls that seek to judge. Open handed in our willingness to help and give for the work that must be done. Open in our spirits to follow where you lead with the dreams you weave around us. With open doors welcoming any and all who come to seek your shelter. Standing in the open to proclaim your peace with joy and with courage.

October 4

Let us be blessed today with the simple grace of kindness, that in all small ways we give joy to the soul of another. To listen with patience, to affirm with sincerity, to help unbidden, to share with a cheerful spirit. Let us be mindful of these many moments when a chance to love is just a word away, just there in the palm of our hand. Then in our giving we will find what no scholar can discover, the purpose to our place in creation, not the high drama of the search for heaven, but the common compassion of caring when caring is all that is needed.

October 5

Knowledge once received is not wisdom. We learn best not by memorizing what others tell us, but by stretching our minds to discover the meaning of truth as we put it to work in the fields of hope around us. We were made to question. Made to think. Made to test the truth by a Mind that never ceases its endless quest of creation. How sad when some entomb their thoughts in a faith too fragile to wonder. We were made to breathe cleaner air than dust in a museum. Tradition will hold us back if we run too far ahead, but we will never catch the Spirit if all we do is stand still.

October 7

Love's need knows no nationality. No age or gender, no time or place. Our hearts turn to love as surely as a lost soul seeks its home. We are creatures made to thrive when in the embrace, even the single embrace, of love's deep affirmation. Without it we wither, left longing for love as though it were a code we could not decipher. With love we shine in light from within; without love we find only shadow even if standing on life's brightest stage. Let your love be known. Say it. Share it. Give it and give it clearly that another spirit may live in love as love lives in you.

October 8

False promises, easy answers, hearing what we want to hear, seeing what we want to see. We have all followed the shortcut deeper into the woods. We all have a story to tell, though the memory shames us to silence. How could we have been so foolish? The spiritual life is not pretending we have never gone astray. It is learning from those mistakes and growing stronger in spite of them. It is giving thanks for the rescue of common sense. We are veterans of the wrong turn, you and me, but wiser guides now on our way home along the bright paths of freedom.

October 9

Waiting is the hard part. Waiting for the test results. Waiting for the phone to ring. Waiting for someone special to come home, for news about the job, for the house to be bought or sold, for the medicine to take effect, for the prayer to be answered. I cannot avoid the waiting game anymore than you, but I can be there with you, to keep watch till time has come, until you know what will happen. My prayers will be with you. My strength joined to yours. Waiting is the hard part, but waiting alone harder still. I will wait with you, until dawn has broken and the night steals away.

October 10

P lease let me introduce myself. You may have heard of me, but perhaps what you have heard is that I am narrow-minded, judgmental and think science is the work of the Devil. You see, I am a person of faith. Not the kind that makes the headlines, but the kind that tries to love others without judgment, to create community with fairness, to explore life for meaning, to listen in order to learn, to value wisdom as shared truth, to be accountable for the trust given me, to be humble enough to know I am neither alone in this universe nor the center of it. Nice to meet you.

October 11

I have some never-prayers, God. Please never let me grow too old to lose the delight of a child's imagination, never too disappointed in life to stop believing each morning is a new beginning, never too concerned with my own burdens to fail to help another whose needs are so clear and pressing, never so busy making a living that I forget what living is about, never so certain that I have all the answers that I stop enjoying the questions, never with so much to say that I don't be still and listen, never so far from you that I do not hear your voice when you call me home.

October 12

Here is an altar call, sent out to any who would receive it, sent out along the electronic pews, streaming amid the masses, an invitation in digital time, post-modern in all but meaning. Please come forward, if you feel so called. Rise up, stand up, be lifted up, from the now that you know, from what holds you down or back, or from what fails to hold you at all through these cold dark nights. Please come forward, into the warmth of an everlasting love, into hope and healing, into something far more real than these tiny screens can convey. Please. Come. Forward. To God.

October 14

Life-line. Sometimes we need a life-line, a rope tossed into a stormy sea, something to cling to, a way out, a way back, a thread to follow to safety. I know this is true because I have been there. I imagine you have too. If so, then you know how critical our care for others can be. We may, through our faith and prayer, be the lifeline for another. Therefore I ask that we all receive grace to be faithful to our calling: casting our prayers out into the dark sea, daring to hope against all odds, pulling with all our might, to bring another soul to shore, another life to peace untroubled.

October 15

There is a garden beyond the shadows, a place of rest and renewal. You may not be able to see it yet, not through the swirl of things that cloud your vision, but it is there. And in time you will get there. You will step through the darkness to the light just on the other side of sorrow. You will find what you are looking for, what you need. I do not say this because I am trying to make you feel better. Right now the only thing that will make you feel better is hope. I say the truth and that truth is your first glimpse of the garden beyond the shadows. The hope is up to you.

October 16

The holy life is not lived in isolation, in sterile conditions of religious purity, where everyone agrees and everyone gets along. Conformity is the death of creativity. Instead it is lived in the noisy marketplace of ideas and opinions, amid the many smells and sounds of our common humanity, the exhilarating and frustrating reality of being alive in the midst of life. If our fingernails are not dirty then we probably have not been practicing our religion. If our faith has not entertained a question we probably have not been thinking. Welcome to the holy chaos of God.

October 17

I am not worthy of love. I have thought that. I am not worthy of any more than I receive, living in the half-light, toiling away beside the conveyor belt that takes good things to others whose lives are so much richer than mine, so much more real and meaningful. I get what I deserve. I have thought all of that when I lived without the word that liberates every heart and lifts up every soul and proclaims with a shout of acclamation heard all the way to heaven: yes, you are worthy! You are the delight of God, the beloved of the source of love, worthy just as you are.

October 18

There are days when I decide to declare a holiday for my spirit. This is one of those days. I have popped the cork of my soul, sending my worries out of the top of my head like multi-colored confetti. I have given my issues a rest, my needs a break, my longings a long longed for release. Today joy runs rampant among the piles of paper that once hemmed in my life, playing tag with freedom and fun. Laughter fills the coffers of my heart and peace provides the music. If we are making too much noise then please come join the party. You will be more than welcome.

October 19

May God's healing mercy find you, wherever you may be, in good days or bad, in places of peace or peril, may it seek you out, discover you and surprise you by its presence. May you feel sustained by this grace, strengthened and supported. May you breathe in the assurance of God's holy protection, drawing it in to the innermost parts of your body and spirit, until you are filled with hope, healed from within, a whole creation within yourself, a source of healing for others. May God's healing mercy find you, and having found you, may it abide, abide and never depart.

October 21

Please, God, keep me ever mindful. Do not let me see the beauty of a sunset without thinking of how precious this Earth is to me and how I must care for her in all that I do. Do not let me pass by a person who seems homeless without renewing my resolve to turn my compassion toward acts of justice. Do not let me walk into my own home without giving thanks for the gift of friends and family. Do not let me come to my place of worship without understanding that it would not exist without my help and stewardship. In all things, dear God, keep me ever mindful.

October 22

Tis a gift to be simple, but tis also a challenge. We live in a society that drives us to consume, not conserve. We are seduced to serve the cult of more. Our children learn early on to want the newest thing. We admire those who have the most. The expensive is the mark of worth, education a tool to get, not a gift to learn. Our own tower of Babel is built not with bricks, but with designer labels. Against this tide it is hard to hold to simplicity, but that is our calling. For if we cannot convince others to live lightly on the Earth, the Earth itself will not be enough to satisfy our hunger.

October 23

We will not pass this way again, but the marks of our life will linger. Our deeds will ripple out through memory, leaving their impression on the souls of all those we knew, some only in passing, but deeply for those who were nearest to us in the ancient dance of emotion. Those marks may stain the lives of others, a source of sorrow, a seed of guilt, or they may so color the sky of another's hopes that they are a rainbow of love left for generations. Let us each choose well the memories we leave in our wake, the handprints we press upon the hearts who hold us dear.

October 24

Y ou Are Here. That's what the directory map at large malls or theme parks tells us. It points to our location. That is also what God tells us sometimes when we pray. Where am I in life, O God, and what am I to do? You are here, says the Lord. Here, in this spot, in this place, at this time, for a reason. The rest is up to you. It makes me smile. Usually. Other times it makes me frustrated. But the simple truth of it has the ring of honesty: we are where we are for a purpose. We are located on the map of life to find our way.

October 25

S peak as if you were in the presence of the Teacher. In every situation, handle your words with care, as if they might break and in breaking send splinters of pain into the heart of another. Do not let passion rule your language, but the cool hand of reason. No argument is ever won by shouting others into silence. No joke that demeans ever worth repeating. If words become blows it is your own soul that will take the beating. Practice the self-discipline of sacred speech, aware of all you share, for the One who created with a Word watches how you speak, and hears all that you say.

October 26

I have kept the night watch for you, whispering hope through the long hours, the dark hours, until the first almost unseen hints of the new day emerge from the shadows to smile the promise of new beginnings. I have no magic gift to tell you that my prayers for you conjured your need to fulfillment, but I can tell you that I was not alone as I prayed. A Spirit moved around me. A Life breathed near me. A Mind far deeper than any thought I will ever have shared the night with me and listened to my simple appeal and flies even now to find you.

October 28

Blessed are the parents who do not over schedule their children for they are the last patrons of playfulness. Blessed are the religious who do not demonize other faiths for they keep open the bridges of understanding. Blessed are the stewards of creation for they are defending the last meadows of Eden. Blessed are the citizens who do not fall prey to political rant for they are the keepers of democracy. Blessed are the romantics who still hold hands more than text for they are lights of an older love. Blessed are the dreamers for they still see what many have never known.

October 29

It began long ago with a single psalm that came to me and has never yet departed: for God alone my soul in silence waits. Those words released many words, here in the quiet hours, the silent hours, when I rise to sit with the rosary of prayer, counting the faces that come before me, each precious in the sight of God, every need, every hope, every moment a mystery of grace unfolding. Then in the silence I see through the candle flame as if through a glass darkly, the language writes itself in this unlikely sanctuary, the prayer becomes its own answer.

October 30

It all begins with small numbers. A few more drops of precipitation, a little more wind, a slight rise in the sea level, a couple of degrees difference in the elevation of the moon. Great forces are born in small numbers, in the increments of existence, the mathematics of our physical being. And as with the natural, so the spiritual. A tiny bit more kindness, a single hope, a small increase in giving, a few more prayers, another moment of patience. Great souls are not instant in being, but being made up of instants. Life without and within, lived in the small things that count.

October 31

In the tradition of Native America, we speak not only of the good news, but of the good medicine. This medicine is the power of the sacred to heal our lives, to put right whatever may be wrong for us. It is the spiritual force of love. Good medicine is both a presence in our lives and an active energy that moves like the Spirit around us. Today I pray that my ancestors may share their good medicine with each of you. I pray that the Creator, the source of all good medicine, may release its authority into your life and through you pass it's healing to touch those you love.

NOVEMBER

November 1

I have forgiveness glowing on the palm of my hand, as though I were holding a small sun, a living light so bright and so warm it could lift life from seeds, pulling life out of the cold dark earth, raising it on green shoots to breathe the air and wave in the wind with shouts of gladness, gladness born of forgiveness, of knowing that mistakes are not a grave that can hold us, but that light can open the tomb of sorrow and bring us back to the chance, the chance to do better, to be better, to become better than we have ever been. I have all of this, right there, in the palm of my hand. Forgiveness.

November 2

I can see into your heart. I can see just how you feel. You are as transparent to me as though you were made of glass. It is not magic, but experience that gives me this gift. I have known you so long and so well that even if you pretend otherwise I know just how you are feeling. It is in your eyes. It is in your hands. How you glance away, how you try so hard to spare me from any worry. I see your soul and watch your thoughts gather like the weather signs of your spirit. I know you as no other ever can. And yet, I said, you still love me. Yes, said my God, and always will.

November 4

I don't watch television so I have been spared most of the political ads, but the other day I was in a hospital waiting room and they had a TV playing that could not be shut off. I have to admit that after sitting through several loops of negative ads I came away not feeling any of the emotions I imagine they wanted me to feel. I just felt sad. We are better than that. Fear is not the rock on which to build a nation. Neither is anger or suspicion. We are not a democracy because we can tear the other side down, but because we can listen to them. Turn the TV off so you can hear.

November 5

God bless all those who must rebuild their lives in the wake of the great storm, Sandy. Give them courage and comfort, strength and support, hope and healing. And let our prayers and gifts for them remind us all of how fragile our lives can be, how quickly what we think we have may be swept away. Open our hearts to one another. Whether we are from Jersey or Japan, do not let disaster be something we face alone, but something that brings the best from us, the dignity of a shared humanity, the compassion of one great family, the faith of a people standing together.

November 6

Dear Mr. President (whoever you may be), welcome to your moment to make history, not as you may imagine, but as your people dream. Hear the truth so you may speak the truth. We will not win our future with war. No citizen will be worth respect unless all citizens are respected equally. All the gold will be worthless if the Earth is left to perish. If we will not educate our children or care for our sick we will not be able to achieve anything of value. Work is not about the profits of the few but the dignity of the many. Faith is not a slogan but a bridge.

November 7

Don't stop now. You have come so far and seen so much. You have weathered storms of the soul and shipwrecked dreams and lost chances and all the what might have beens of youth. You have accomplished more than you even know and done what no other could do and made life a joy for so many they cannot be counted. You have graced this life. You have blessed this life. You are unique. And for all the scars you think you wear, you are more beautiful than sunrise. Don't stop now. There is so much more for you to be and so many surprises just around the corner.

November 8

Yesterday I sat with an elder of the Cherokee people and listened to the chant of the human beings, an ancient hymn that reminds us to honor The One Who Provides All Things each day. You have to dream up yourself again, the elder said. You have to fly like the geese who know that if you travel together no wind to the contrary can hold you back. I am so grateful to be able to listen and learn. I am so glad that my faith is open to new wisdom and different voices. If I lived in a religious closet I would have missed this elder's song, missed a chance to dream myself again, missed the wild call to fly.

November 9

Be my shadow, God, stay with me where ever I may go. I do not ask that you stand before me, for I can face what I need to do and take responsibility for the choices I make. But let me feel you at my shoulder, let me know you have my back, let me find strength in your presence at my side. I am not afraid. I take up my life in both hands and walk the sacred way. I know times of struggle and hours of grace, I carry both burdens and hope together. I am a steward of the freedom you have given me. Only be my shadow, that I may know your light guides my way.

November 11

God bless our veterans, those who went, those who returned, those who did not make it home. Bless them for their sacrifice, bless them for their gift to us, bless them for being faithful. Bless their families, those who know the pain of separation, the long service of anxious waiting. Bless the veterans to be, the young men and women who stand guard now, keep them safe. Bless all who work for peace, help them bring swift the day when all the wars shall cease. And bless the unknown vets, captured or killed, give them your deepest grace, tell them we did not forget.

November 12

Prayer is many things, but one of its most important aspects is that it is a discipline. Yes, prayer can happen spontaneously, but consistent prayer, deeply focused, intentional prayer: that requires a willingness to shape the spiritual life. Prayer is exercise. It repeats a spiritual motion in order to become stronger. It creates a pattern that becomes a place in itself, a state of being that is within reality, but separate, set aside as a sacred space, a holy ground where the heart rises to meet the mind. Prayer is energy, released not at random, but through channels that change lives.

November 13

Enter quietly now this season of your heart, this time of colder winds and falling leaves, when old memories burn like wood smoke on the breeze, when what is to come is buried in the sleeping earth all around you. Listen to the crisp air as it rattles the old bone branches. There is a message here for you, something you know by instinct, the hint of mortality, the whisper of age. Let these autumn twilights speak your language, let them have their say, for this is the changing time, the season of your heart, when God covers you with warming wings before the snow can find you.

November 14

I dreamed about my little dog again last night. She was with me for twenty years before she passed away some time ago. I still think about her and often dream of her. In my tradition we speak of animals as more than our companions. They have a spirit they share with us, a wisdom and presence, a gift of deep grace. I think many of you know that and have experienced it for yourselves. Join me in prayer for all those living friends around us. Join me in being dedicated to their protection, respect and care. How diminished we are without them, how blessed we are by them.

November 15

What would happen? What would happen if I consecrated one day of my life to living as though I were a prayer? If I tried that day to speak with kindness, to think well of every person I met, to bring as much help to others as I could offer? If I gave time to friends and family, a helping hand to my community, a gift to my church or to charity or to any cause that might warm my heart and serve the common good? If I were to carry a word of holy writing within my spirit, studying how it shaped me? If I lived one day in love intentioned, in faith enjoyed? What would happen?

November 16

We got one of those calls yesterday, one of those unexpected calls with news that takes well-ordered life and spins it into a spiral that will not soon come to rest. I think you know what I mean. How quickly an illness or death or sadness breaks into our homes. How quickly they take us by surprise and come to claim our reality like generals commanding a conquering army. Now is the hour of our sorrow, now more than ever our need for faith. Come gentle light of love, come stand before the storm. Come remind us of your power: Death may call, but Life will answer.

November 18

Take up the banner now, the one carried by so many for so long. Lift it up, unfurl it, let all those who can see it clearly. This is your time to carry it, your time to do what others have done before, to make your stand and by so doing to be the standard of vision for all who will gather beside you. We need you now, we all need you, because we need the message you will carry. For too long our people have been divided, despairing that they will never see again the truth held high to heal them. Take up the banner: Justice In Jerusalem, Peace In All The World.

November 19

Sometimes I laugh when I pray, I hope you do too. So often prayer is such a serious business, with so many deep needs and heartfelt petitions, but there are those moments, those rare and happy times, when the thanksgivings start to flow like a mountain stream rushing over rocks, life running to dance in sunlight. And I cannot help but smile, smile at the beauty of it all, smile in grace so abundant. May God give you reason to laugh today. May your prayers turn to delight. May your thanks be said with a smile. May your life run like a stream to catch the sunlight before you.

November 20

You are not lost. Not to me. And never will be. No matter where you may be, no matter how far or deep or dark or empty or alone or confusing or new or complex or tangled or bad or difficult, I will find you. I will find you and I will be with you. I will come to you and hold you and care for you and uplift you and protect you and heal you and save you and bring you home. So you never need be afraid. Never. For you will not be lost, not to me. I have you. Now and forever. Be at peace and rest in that peace. You will never be in a place my love cannot find. So says our God.

November 21

Outside the windows where I pray is a small shrine of Mary, weathered wood gone gray from rain and snow, standing quietly along an old fence, the kind of roadside marker travelers once saw as they made their way along dusty roads or windswept passes. It is to Mary that my heart turns as I pause to pray for all who travel. Watch over them, dear Mary, keep them safe as they go, around the block, around the world, full of anticipation, moving through their story in search of a new memory: bless the travelers on their journey and bring them gently home.

November 22

Today I give thanks for all indigenous people. For our ancestors who came before, who endured every hardship, who gave us life like a precious ember guarded against the harsh winds of history. For our elders who speak wisdom into silence, who show us how to live in dignity the ancient virtues that are our only path forward. For our families. For our youth. For our children. I thank God for you today, each and every one, and fast this day that it may be holy, a day of remembrance, for what you gave and give.

November 23

Ten reasons you know you go to the right church: 1. You don't cringe when you read about it in the news; 2. You do cringe but you keep going anyway; 3. You don't take its clergy too seriously; 4. You have gone long enough to have a favorite place to sit; 5. You pledge your dollars to support it; 6. You look forward to its pot luck suppers; 7. You know at least one other person you wish could discover it; 8. You have hymns you really love; 9. You miss it if you are away; 10. You don't believe it is the exclusive elevator to heaven.

November 25

Open your heart and you will open your mind. Fear subverts faith. Knowledge overcomes fear. The more that we come to know one another as brothers and sisters, no matter how different we may seem, the more we create peace and possibility. The challenge before us is to dare to listen. To step out from our bunkers into the open spaces between ourselves, as dangerous as that may seem, and encounter one another as we are. The other is us. The human family is our birthright. We are diverse by design. Open your heart and you will open your mind.

November 26

Dear God, since most of my prayers turn into a shopping list, I thought I would just own up and leave you one. Please don't think me rude. These really are things I need. When you get a chance, please pick up some more hope. I always seem to need that. And some extra love. Faith, patience and humor: the staples. Get me a little courage if you would, to make the tough calls when they come around. I could use a generous amount of wisdom but I will get by with what you can spare. And time, please. Just enough. To put this list to good use. Thank you, dear God, I am grateful.

November 27

Listen to the wind. It has something to tell you. Whether it is as still, as quiet, as the current that lifts the hawk to circle the sky or as strong, as loud, as the sea breeze chasing the high waves to shore: the wind has something to say. I believe there is a word for each of us, a message sent directly to us, that flows through the celestial channels every day, offering us insight and vision, clarity and creative ideas, if only we will stop long enough to receive it. Be still. Be awake. Trust your spiritual senses. Listen to the wind. God is speaking to you.

November 28

God bless all of you who never quite fit, never quite learned the marching orders, never dressed or talked or thought or believed or acted just like all the others. God bless all the square pegs, the odd ones out, the quirky, artistic, dreamy, visionary, strange and creative people who make this world such a much more interesting place to be. Without you we would be a mannequin parade of what is expected, not a dance of what is possible. Swim on against the tide. Listen to that different drum. Be who God gifted you to be and let your light be brighter still for its unique color.

November 29

Come rest beside me. Come sit beneath the shade of my prayer. Catch your breath. Put down your burdens. I know how much you have carried, both for yourself and others. I know how faithful you are, how responsible, how much like the silent servant who moves behind the scenes cleaning up the endless needs of family. But if you do not stop sometimes, if you do not give your own heart time to heal, you will not shepherd your hopes to the answer you have sought so long. Come rest beside me. I will keep watch until you need to lift love upon your strong shoulder.

November 30

Random grace gathers around me, like starlight reflected on water, brief glimpses of light, pure joy for those who will receive it. Work for the one who has been looking for so long, at last good news about a job. Hope for a young person with troubles at home, a path to follow that leads to friends who care. Healing for an addiction, healing for an illness, healing for a broken dream. Renewal for the tired soul, patience for the one who keeps watch. All these small graces are in the air, lights dancing in darkness. Let prayer draw them to those for whom they are intended.

DECEMBER

December 2

Come let us renew our vow to serve the cause of justice. Let us set aside all outer trappings of place and privilege, the politics we wear like costumes of hope, and see one another as we are, a family held together by bonds of shared story stronger than any partisan loyalty. Let our common resolve turn to those whose need is clear, the silent ones who wait beneath the shadows of war, the hungry ones who cry for enough to eat, the children used, the women abused, the whole multitude that watches what we do. Come let us be what they pray we will be before time steals our honor.

December 3

This is the season for believing, the time to look ahead in expectation, to climb the hill to see who might be coming down the road. This is the season to be awake, to listen to the sounds of the sacred moving around, stirring the dead leaves with the breath of the Spirit. This is the season to make ready, to prepare a place in the heart of hope, to clear the path that leads to a welcoming home. God could sweep in majesty from one end of time to another, but this is the season when God comes to Earth to walk the path that leads to your front door.

D e c e m b e r   4

The Earth puts on her white coat, her winter coat, and drapes the rivers, scarves of blue, around her neck to ward off the chill, the cold air of silent space, as she dances, always dances, turning and turning again, to spin out the long seasons of her life. How beautiful she is in her dance, how beautiful our mother, the Earth, and how worthy of our love and care. May she dance forever, twirl and turn beneath the far flung stars. And may we never cease to honor her as children do, following behind her forest skirts, laughing to try to catch her.

D e c e m b e r   5

May your family be blessed. May the bonds that bind you in love be strengthened. May the lines of communication that let you hear what is felt be clear between you. May the honesty, the trust, and the patience that are the core of your shared lives be renewed. May you be gifted with joyful memories, intriguing new discoveries, and just enough challenge to give you a reason to bend your hearts toward a common goal. May healing find haven in your home. May peace abide among you. Large or small, near or far, of any shape or number: may your family be blessed.

December 6

The answer was right before us all the time. We searched the heavens for the clue. We dug through ancient books dusty with age and arcane in meaning. We followed prophets and philosophers and politicians, thinking one of them might know the truth. We tried piety. We tried pleasure. Neither was the key. And then the Teacher showed us, not in lofty words or stern laws, but in the eyes of a child. Look deeply into those eyes. See innocence. See trust. See a soul still open to the wildness of wonder. Here is your answer, the Teacher said, right before you all the time.

December 7

We have a job to do, you and I, and all those called to work beside us, a team of workers, a community sent out to labor together for a common goal, set a task and asked to be faithful to it. We are the stewards of mission, the entrusted workers, hired on not for wages, but for vocation, for the love of what we do. We are the skilled workers of love and faith, of mercy and caring, of justice and truth. We have a job to do. Let us be about it with renewed energy and cheerful hearts: making straight the path that peace will take when war is silent and only angels sing.

December 9

G od, please watch over all those for whom this time of year is difficult. For those who mark the anniversary of a loss. For those whose memories are burdens. For those struggling to find work or make ends meet. For those living with depression or grief. For the poor, the homeless, and the hungry. For any person left on the sidelines of a holiday parade. Turn our hearts to show them our love and understanding. Give them comfort and peace. Let the blessings of your light shine where they are most needed. May healing be their gift and hope the song of their quiet season.

December 10

I came cloud walking through empty hallways, past moonlit windows, wrapped against the cold of night, because I heard a voice calling softly, because I knew I was needed. I sent my prayer hours ago, out over a sleeping world, through miles of imagined distance, to find you where you are waiting, waiting for an answer. Be comforted, the prayer said, be at peace in mind and heart. Someone sits through the night with you, someone keeps the watch unseen beside you. I heard you calling in the night, though you never spoke a word or even knew my name.

December 11

If laughter is the best medicine, then let the church be our open all night pharmacy. A place of joy on every corner. A house full of smiles and warm greetings. A welcoming home where you can leave judgment at the door and walk in to find room for everyone. No exclusive club, no finishing school for the saved, but a rowdy hall of happiness where people can laugh as they work together to make the holy happen. Joy is not the denial of sorrow, but the affirmation of hope over hurt, life over death, good over evil. Religion is no joking matter only if we missed the joke.

December 12

You were born to believe. Even if there have been times when you tried to let go of faith, accepting doubts or disappointments as reason to suspend your dreams, you never were able to release that last spark of light within you. It is you. You were born to believe. Against the odds, despite the culture, through the hard work of hope, you have not only kept the faith but given it away. You sing the silence to song. You trust the love around you. You make justice grow. You were born to do this. It is your birthright. It is your calling. It is the part of time entrusted to your care.

D e c e m b e r   1 3

Standing alone at night, beneath a curious moon, I searched for that single star, the one that would be my sign of hope. But instead, I saw a field of stars, cast shimmering across the heavens, a countless sweep of stars, more than I could carry. Hope and you do not hope alone. Love and you do not love alone. Like stars our dreams are cast to high heaven, some to lead us to all we imagined, others only to watch over us on our way, but all shine together, all share the same beauty. We do not pass this way alone, but journey in light, beneath a curious moon.

D e c e m b e r   1 4

I have seen famous religious leaders whose writings and lives I have admired for years. I have seen worship services great and small that have moved me with deep joy and reverence. I have seen sacred places where generations of people have made the ground holy with their devotion. I have seen natural moments in Earth, sea and sky that have left me breathless in wonder and awe. But I have never seen anything that made me more sure of what I believe than the sight of a single person alone in an empty church quietly praying.

December 16

Sometimes our hearts cannot bear the pain, our minds cannot encompass the meaning, the random hurt so cruel, the senseless loss too staggering for language to express. Our souls stand mute, the thousand mile stare, seeking an answer to the haunted question, why? The harm we do we do to ourselves, but the love we give we give to all. Peace now to those who have passed, peace to those who remain. Hold those you love a little tighter. Do not be resigned, but resolved to love more deeply. Let the laughter of children call us all from the daze of sorrow to where they play in light unceasing.

December 17

On a cold winter's morning, when it was still dark and the whole town was huddled against the night, an old man climbed a hill by lantern light. He walked against the wind, not minding the steep and twisted path, until he came to the top. He stopped to rest, looking out at the still sleeping world around him. Then summoning all his strength he drew in a great breath of chilly air and shouted "Yes!" into the darkness. His voice echoed over the frozen land, causing the ice to fall from houses, the snow from trees. "Yes", he cried. Yes to life. Yes to love. And dawn broke over his valley.

December 18

Come, Emmanuel, now is the time of our need. Come and bind up our confidence, so shaken beneath uncertain skies, and lift us up to walk with you, where paths make sense and seem to lead us home. Come remind us of our early dreams, the ones once followed like stars, and give us the will to live them, to be the light for others. Come sing to us the ancient songs of our season, the sounds that set our spirits to soar above shadows, that we may breathe the clean air of heaven. Come, Emmanuel, for now is the time when we are needed, needed as never before.

December 19

Did you think you had been forgotten? I know it is not like you to admit it if you did. That's not your spiritual style. But I also know that as you stand in the midst of so much activity, so many different ways that you are plugged into the lives of others, so often that you give all that you can to keep the wheels turning for others, you cannot help but wonder if anyone notices you in the dust of life around you. Freeze frame your busy world for just this second and hear my voice clearly: you are never forgotten. What you do for love, Love knows. Love sees. Love remembers.

December 20

The candles where I pray flicker to life one-by-one, each a small universe of hope in itself, bravely aflame with the desire to be fulfilled, glowing against the dark as if saying I am here. I am here, let me live. I am here, let me dream, let me grow, let me become. I light my candles because they embody not only the prayers but the person. They are the spark of life within each of us, flickering within the unseen air of the Spirit, shining a tiny beacon into the cold expanse of space, repeating the ancient message of our heartbeats: I am here.

December 21

Sin is the negative space of the sacred. What we hold sacred, we cherish, we protect, we nurture. In an ethical vacuum where nothing is sacred, we are much more likely to abuse what we would otherwise honor. As the borders of the sacred diminish, the empire of sorrow expands. The work of faith is the restoration of the sacred. We must help others to discover the value of life in everything around them: in people who are different, in everyday encounters, in the Earth itself. We must grow the sacred. We must fill in the blank spaces with reverence and the empty spaces with respect.

December 23

Three wise women set out to follow the star. Each ended the journey and gave away her treasure along the way. One dropped out when she was needed to heal the sick during a plague. The second stayed behind to help prevent a war with her leadership. The last remained in a great city to provide for the poor. When the star left the heavens each awoke the next day to discover a gift placed beside her while she slept. They never solved this mystery, but the meaning is clear: they had arrived at their destination even though they had not completed their journey.

December 24

What a wonderful thing to be on the eve. On the threshold. On the night before. At the very dawn of something new. It is the linguistic sign of ultimate expectation. It is the spiritual sign of immanent contact with the divine. I pray this day be the eve of your life. May it fill you with the energy of knowing that something new and empowering is about to happen. This is the turning point. This is the hinge time, the moment when reality begins to change. Now is your eve, your countdown to a fresh beginning. What has happened has happened: now hope is at the door.

December 25

Can you hear it? Can you hear the sound of that tiny heartbeat, newborn, gently drumming life back into a cold world? The mystery of God is not to be found in grand ceremonies or great philosophies, not in searching the farthest edge of the universe or diving deeply into the inner caverns of our own consciousness. The essence of all that is holy is in that small sound, that little heartbeat, a new life stirring beneath the covers of history, the child that insists on living despite all the odds. God is in that heartbeat, that newborn life, that miracle within us all.

December 26

In the stillness I wait, in the stillness I listen, patient in prayer, riding the deep currents of faith across an empty sea, sailing beneath a peaceful moon, out to where life becomes only lights, distant and without worry. However hectic your life may seem, however pressured or burdened, I will always have room to carry your soul passenger on my late night voyages. Be at rest today, be comforted and sustained, for every evening an aging sailor sets sail to take your hopes to heaven, sailing out into the stillness, far beyond the shores of cluttered time, beneath a peaceful moon.

December 27

This is the time when people make New Year's resolutions. Here are a few I am considering. I will resolve not to congratulate myself when things go well and blame God when they don't. I will not think too highly of my own faith and too lightly of what others believe. I will find some reason to laugh each day even if I feel like crying. I will tell those I love that I love them as often as I can. I will talk less about saving this planet and do more to make it so. I will practice kindness until I get it right. I will live in grace as if my new year were only one day long. I will be peace.

December 28

A dream brought me to pray. I saw a narrow bridge, a foot path over a wide stream, sturdy built but narrow, a place of both beauty and choice. Here an elder kept watch, bidding travelers to lay down their burdens before crossing the bridge. The vision is simple and clear. Let us leave as much as we can here, on this side of time, before we cross over to tomorrow. Let us come to the end of this year without regrets, worries, fears or anger. Let what needs to be left behind be released that our steps are as light as innocent hope, our hearts as free as first felt love.

December 30

Don't wait. If you want to make some spiritual changes in your life in the days to come, maybe these two little words can help. They are a simple reminder that good things happen when we seize the opportunities God places before us. The wisdom of my rural roots tells me that hardly a day goes by without a chance to be a blessing. So if you have a chance to do something, say something, or be something that you believe you are being called to act on in love then don't wait. Share all that you can when you can and make every day another minute in heaven.

December 31

For two years I have cast my words out, messages in bottles, thrown into the electronic sea. When I began I knew of only a handful of others out there who would read them. Now there are so many more. The sacred is a great mysterious ocean, separating us by our individuality, connecting us by our community, a vast rolling mystery, calling us to stand beside the shores of time, receiving our messages, answering our prayers, reminding us that even in the void when we believe we are castaways of fate, we are never alone. God bless you, friends, for being there.